CHECKS AND BALANCES
IN THE U.S. GOVERNMENT

The Judicial Branch
Evaluating and Interpreting Laws

EDITED BY BRIAN DUIGNAN AND CAROLYN DECARLO

Britannica
Educational Publishing

IN ASSOCIATION WITH

ROSEN
EDUCATIONAL SERVICES

Published in 2019 by Britannica Educational Publishing (a trademark of Encyclopædia Britannica, Inc.) in association with The Rosen Publishing Group, Inc.
29 East 21st Street, New York, NY 10010

Distributed exclusively by Rosen Publishing.
To see additional Britannica Educational Publishing titles, go to rosenpublishing.com.

Britannica Educational Publishing
J.E. Luebering: Executive Director, Core Editorial
Andrea R. Field: Managing Editor, Compton's by Britannica

Rosen Publishing
Carolyn DeCarlo: Editor
Nelson Sá: Art Director
Brian Garvey: Series Designer/Book Layout
Cindy Reiman: Photography Manager
Bruce Donnola: Photo Researcher

Library of Congress Cataloging-in-Publication Data

Names: Duignan, Brian, editor. | DeCarlo, Carolyn, editor.
Title: The judicial branch : evaluating and interpreting laws / edited by Brian Duignan and Carolyn DeCarlo.
Description: New York : Britannica Educational Publishing, in Association with Rosen Publishing, 2019. | Series: Checks and balances in the U.S. government | Includes bibliographical references and index. | Audience: Grades 7-12.
Identifiers: LCCN 2017056243| ISBN 9781538301678 (library bound : alk. paper) | ISBN 9781538301685 (pbk. : alk. paper)
Subjects: LCSH: Courts—United States—Juvenile literature. | Civil rights—United States—Juvenile literature. | Law—United States—Interpretation and construction—Juvenile literature. | Justice, Administration of—United States—Juvenile literature.
Classification: LCC KF8720 .J83 2018 | DDC 347.73/2—dc23
LC record available at https://lccn.loc.gov/2017056243

Manufactured in the United States of America

CONTENTS

The judiciary is the branch of government whose task is the authoritative adjudication (or, resolution) of controversies over the application of laws in specific situations. Conflicts brought before the judiciary are embodied in cases involving litigants, who may be individuals, groups, legal entities (e.g., corporations), or governments and their agencies. Conflicts that allege personal or financial harm resulting from violations of law or binding legal agreements between litigants—other than violations legally defined as crimes—produce civil cases. Judicial decisions in civil cases often require the losing or offending party to pay financial compensation to the winner. Crimes produce criminal cases, which are officially defined as conflicts between the state or its citizens and the accused (defendant) rather than as conflicts between the victim of the crime and the defendant. Judicial decisions in criminal cases determine whether the accused is guilty or not guilty. A defendant found guilty is sentenced to punishments, which may involve the payment of a fine, a term of imprisonment, or, in the most serious cases in some legal systems, state-imposed physical mutilation or even death.

Judiciaries also frequently resolve administrative cases, disputes between individuals, groups, or legal entities and government agencies over the application of laws or the implementation of government programs. Most legal systems have incorporated the principle of state sovereignty, whereby governments may not be sued by nonstate litigants without their consent. This principle limits the right of litigants to pursue remedies against government actions. Nevertheless, the right of citizens to be free from the arbitrary, improper, or abusive application of laws and government regulations has long been recognized and is the focus of administrative cases.

Legal systems differ in the extent to which their judiciaries handle civil, criminal, and administrative cases. In some, courts hear all three kinds of disputes. In others there are specialized civil, criminal, and administrative courts. Still others have some general and some specialized courts.

In many cases the conflicts that are brought to courts for resolution are uncontested. The majority of civil cases in the United States—such as those involving divorce, child custody, or the interpretation of contracts— are settled out of court and never go to trial. The same is true for criminal cases in the United States, where the practice of extrajudicial plea bargaining is used extensively. The different criminal process that characterizes the United Kingdom and civil-law countries makes plea bargaining of the sort practiced in the United States less likely—or

A lawyer addresses a jury in a traditional U.S. courtroom.

even officially impossible. In cases of plea bargaining the court's function is administrative, limited to officially ratifying and recording the agreement the parties have reached out of court.

When the judiciary does decide a controversy, a body of regulations governs what parties are allowed before the court, what evidence will be admitted, what trial procedure will be followed, and what types of judgments may be rendered. Judicial proceedings involve the participation of a number of people. Although the judge is the central figure, along with the parties to the controversy and the lawyers who represent them, there are other individuals involved, including witnesses, clerks, bailiffs, administrators, and jurors when the proceeding involves a jury.

CHAPTER ONE

THE JUDICIARY IN PERSPECTIVE

The stated function of the courts is the authoritative adjudication of controversies over the application of laws in specific situations. However, it is unavoidable that courts also make law and public policy, because judges must exercise at least some measure of discretion in deciding which litigant claims are legally correct or otherwise most appropriate. Lawmaking and policy making by courts are most evident when powerful national supreme courts (e.g., those in the United States, Germany, and India) exercise their power of judicial review to hold laws or major government actions unconstitutional. They also can occur, however, when judiciaries are behaving as administrators, even when they are merely ratifying agreements reached out of court. Patterns of settlement for suits between employers and employees may be more favourable to employees than formal law would seem to require, because they are influenced by de facto changes in the law that may result from the decisions by juries or trial judges who may regularly be more sympathetic to workers. Formal laws regulating child custody or financial settlements in divorce cases can similarly be altered over time as juries process the claims of the litigants before them in persistent ways.

POWER AND RISK

Legal scholars are fond of quoting the maxim that courts have neither the "power of the purse nor of the sword," meaning that they, unlike other institutions of government, rarely have the power to raise and spend money and do not command the institutions of coercion (the police and the military). Without force or monetary inducements, courts are weak institutions, because they are denied the most efficacious means of ensuring that their decisions are complied with and enforced. In fact, the enforcement of such orders is carried out by the executive branch and may require funding from the legislative branch.

The most significant powers of courts come from their institutional legitimacy. An institution is legitimate when it is perceived as having the right or the authority to make decisions and when its decisions are viewed as worthy of respect or obedience. Judicial legitimacy derives from the belief that judges are impartial and that their decisions are grounded in law, not ideology and politics. Often in sharp contrast to other political institutions (such as legislatures), courts are respected—indeed often revered—because their decisions are viewed as being principled rather than motivated by self-interest or partisanship. To the extent that courts are perceived as legitimate by their constituents, their decisions—even their unpopular ones—are respected, acquiesced to, and accepted.

The justices of the U.S. Supreme Court, for example, often make reference to legitimacy as one of the institution's most precious (and perhaps most volatile) resources. Justices have asserted that frequent reversals of existing precedents undermine the legitimacy of the judiciary. Others have argued that some issues (e.g., the president's war-making powers) are simply too politically sensitive for courts to intervene in. If courts become embroiled in ordinary political disputes and are seen as just another

The nine current U.S. Supreme Court judges include (*left to right*) Ruth Bader Ginsburg, Elena Kagan, Anthony M. Kennedy, Samuel Alito, Jr., John G. Roberts, Sonia Sotomayor, Clarence Thomas, Neil Gorsuch, and Stephen Breyer.

political actor trying to advance its ideology, interests, and preferences, then the legitimacy of the institution can be gravely damaged. Some have argued that just this kind of damage was done when the U.S. Supreme Court intervened in the 2000 presidential election and, ultimately, determined the winner. In general, judges are mindful of threats to the legitimacy of the courts and are unwilling to put it at risk in order to prevail in any particular political or legal controversy.

Courts are not naturally and universally endowed with legitimacy; rather, a sense of legitimacy is accrued and built over time. Throughout the world, the decisions of courts have often been ignored or violently opposed. In some countries, unpopular rulings have resulted in riots (Bulgaria); court buildings have been attacked and burned (Pakistan); judges have been intimidated and removed from office (Zimbabwe), assassinated (Uganda), or reassigned to courts in the hinterland (Japan); courts have been stripped of their jurisdiction (United States); and, in the most extreme cases, judicial institutions have been suspended (United States) or abolished (Russia).

JUDICIAL OFFICE

In common-law countries, such as the United States, the path to judicial office typically begins with a significant amount of time in the private practice of law or, less commonly, in law teaching or governmental legal service before

COMMON LAW OR CIVIL LAW?

Common law, also called Anglo-American law, is the body of customary law, based upon judicial decisions and embodied in reports of decided cases, that has been administered by the common-law courts of England since the Middle Ages. From it has evolved the type of legal system now found also in the United States and in most of the member states of the Commonwealth (formerly the British Commonwealth of Nations). In this sense, common law, practiced throughout the United States (except in Louisiana, which utilizes civil law) stands in contrast to the legal system derived from civil law, now widespread in continental Europe and elsewhere.

In civil-law systems, judges apply principles embodied in statutes, or law codes, rather than relying on precedents established in earlier cases. Used in another sense, the term "civil law" refers to the law that governs the private relations between individuals or businesses, as distinguished from the law that applies to criminal matters.

becoming a judge. Judges are appointed or elected to office; there is no competitive examination. In England, the appointive system prevails for all levels of judges, including even lay magistrates. Appointments are made by a Judicial

Appointments Commission (subject to approval by the lord chancellor). Judges are kept surprisingly free from party politics. In the United States, the appointive method is used in federal courts and some state courts, but ideological and partisan considerations—particularly at the federal level—play a very significant role in appointments to the bench. In the United States, all appointments to the federal bench, and many appointments to the state judiciary, are made by the chief executive (president or governor), though these appointments are generally subject to legislative approval. In many states, however, judges are popularly elected, sometimes on nonpartisan ballots, sometimes on partisan ballots with all the trappings of traditional political contests.

A third method of judicial selection, devised in an attempt to de-emphasize partisan considerations (and to give more power to the organized bar) while maintaining some measure of popular control over the selection of judges, has grown in popularity. Called the Missouri Plan, it involves the

Portraits of U.S. chief justices John Jay, John Rutledge, Oliver Ellsworth, John Marshall, Roger B. Taney, Salmon P. Chase, Morrison R. Waite, and Melville W. Fuller.

creation of a nominating commission that screens judicial candidates and submits to the appointing authority a limited number of names of persons considered qualified. The appointing authority must select from the list submitted. The person chosen as judge then assumes office for a limited time and, after the conclusion of this probationary period, stands for "election" for a much longer term. The judge does not run against any other candidate; rather, he is judged only against his own record. The ballot, called a retention ballot, often simply reads "Shall Judge X be retained?" In practice, few judges are removed from office through retention ballots. These different selection systems strike different balances between the principles of democratic accountability and judicial independence.

In common-law countries, a person does not necessarily enter the judiciary at a low level; he may be appointed or elected to the country's highest court or to one of its intermediate courts without any prior judicial experience. Indeed, even courtroom experience is not a prerequisite for a judgeship in the United States. There is also no regular pattern of promotion, and judges are not assured of a long tenure with ultimate retirement on a pension. In some courts, life tenure is provided, sometimes subject to mandatory retirement at a fixed age. In others, tenure is limited to a stated term of years. At the conclusion of his term, if not mandatorily retired earlier, the judge must be reelected or reappointed if he is to continue.

THE CHIEF JUSTICE

The chief justice of the United States is the presiding judge in the Supreme Court of the United States and the highest judicial officer of the nation. The chief justice is appointed by the president with the advice and consent of the Senate and has life tenure. His primary functions are to preside over the Supreme Court in its public sessions when the court is hearing arguments and during its private conferences when it is discussing and deciding cases. He serves as chairman in the court and has authority to assign the writing of opinions in cases where he is a member of the majority; otherwise his powers are the same as those of any other Supreme Court justice. The chief justice customarily administers the oath of office to the president and vice president at the time of their inauguration. The chief justice is also the presiding officer of the Judicial Conference of the United States, an assembly of judges

Chief Justice John G. Roberts, Jr., was nominated to the U.S. Supreme Court in 2005 by then-President George W. Bush.

representing all the federal courts that reviews and investigates problems relating to the administration of justice in those courts.

When the office is occupied by a person of extraordinary intellectual capacity and dynamic personality, as was the case with John Marshall (served 1801–35), the chief justice may exert a great influence on the court's work. When the occupant of the centre chair is a lesser figure, as has often been the case, he is likely to be overshadowed by other members of the court.

The title of chief justice is also usually accorded the presiding judicial officer within any multi-judge court, as well as to the highest judicial officer within a state of the United States. In the United Kingdom, the title of lord chief justice of England is held by the head of the judiciary of England and Wales.

PROCEDURES FOR REMOVAL

While in office, common-law judges enjoy greater power and prestige and more independence than their civil-law counterparts. A common-law judge, who occupies a position to which most members of the legal profession aspire, is not subject to outside supervision and inspection by any council of judges or by a minister of justice; nor is he liable to be transferred by such an official from court to court or from place to place. The only administrative control over common-law judges is exercised by judicial colleagues, whose powers of management are generally slight, being limited to matters such as requiring periodic reports of pending cases and arranging for temporary (and usually consensual) transfers of judges between courts when factors such as illness or congested calendars require them. Only judges who misbehave very badly (e.g., by abusing their office) are in danger of disciplinary sanctions, and then usually only by way of criminal prosecution for the alleged misdeeds or by legislative impeachment and trial, resulting in removal from office—a very cumbersome, slow, ill-defined, inflexible, ineffective, and seldom-used procedure. Some parts of the United States have developed more expeditious methods of judicial discipline, in which senior judges are vested with the power to impose sanctions on erring colleagues ranging from reprimand to removal from office. They are also vested with the power to retire judges who have become physically or mentally unfit to discharge their duties.

In the United States, the ultimate act of discipline is impeachment. Federal judges may be removed from office based upon an impeachment by the House of Representatives and a conviction by the Senate. Very few judges have been either impeached or convicted (one associate justice of the Supreme Court, Samuel Chase, was impeached but was not convicted). In other parts of the world, including Latin America, impeachment has been institutionalized. In Argentina, for example, a magistrate council investigates judicial misconduct and may remove judges from office.

Except at the very highest appellate level, common-law judges are no less subject than their civil-law counterparts to appellate reversals of their judgments. But appellate review cannot fairly be regarded as discipline. It is designed to protect the rights of litigants; to clarify, expound, and develop the law; and to help and guide lower-court judges, not to reprimand them.

CHAPTER TWO

JUDICIAL REVIEW

Judicial review is the power of the courts of a country to examine the actions of the legislative, executive, and administrative arms of the government and to determine whether such actions are consistent with the constitution. Actions judged inconsistent are declared unconstitutional and, therefore, null and void. The institution of judicial review in this sense depends upon the existence of a written constitution.

CONSTITUTIONAL REVIEW

The conventional usage of the term "judicial review" could be more accurately described as constitutional review, because there also exists a long practice of judicial review of the actions of administrative agencies that require neither that courts have the power to declare those actions unconstitutional nor that the country have a written constitution. Constitutional judicial review is usually considered to have begun with the assertion by John Marshall, chief justice of the United States (1801–35), in *Marbury*

v. *Madison* (1803), that the Supreme Court of the United States had the power to invalidate legislation enacted by Congress. There was, however, no express warrant for Marshall's assertion of the power of judicial review in the actual text of the Constitution of the United States; its success rested ultimately on the Supreme Court's own ruling, plus the absence of effective political challenge to it.

Constitutional judicial review exists in several forms. In countries that follow U.S. practice (e.g., Kenya and New Zealand), judicial review can be exercised only in concrete cases or controversies and only after the fact—i.e., only laws that are in effect or actions that have already occurred can be found to be unconstitutional, and then only when they involve a specific dispute between litigants. In France, judicial review must take place in the abstract (i.e., in the absence of an actual case or controversy) and before promulgation (i.e., before a challenged law has taken effect). In other countries (e.g., Austria, Germany, South Korea, and Spain) courts can exercise judicial review only after a law has taken effect, though they can do so either in the abstract or in concrete cases. Systems of constitutional judicial review also differ in the extent to which they allow courts to exercise it. For example, in the United States all courts have the power to entertain claims of unconstitutionality, but in some countries (e.g., France, Germany, New Zealand, and South Africa) only specialized constitutional courts can hear such claims.

After World War II, many countries felt strong pressure to adopt judicial review as a result of the influence of U.S. constitutional ideas—particularly the idea that a system of constitutional checks and balances is an essential element of democratic government. Some observers concluded that the concentration of government power in the executive, substantially unchecked by other agencies of government, contributed to the rise of totalitarian regimes in Germany and Japan in the era between World War I and World War II. Although judicial review had been relatively uncommon before World War II, by the early 21st century more than 100 countries had specifically incorporated judicial review into their constitutions.

JUDICIAL REVIEW IN THE UNITED STATES

In the U.S. system of judicial review, constitutional questions can be raised only in connection with actual "cases and controversies." Advisory opinions to the government are not rendered by U.S. federal courts. Although the cases and controversies requirement has been relaxed by the Supreme Court—at least to the extent of allowing class-action suits or allowing organizations to sue on behalf of their members who have not personally brought suit—it is still the case that courts will not decide a constitutional question unless it is rooted in a controversy in which the parties have a direct, personal interest. This requirement

MARBURY V. MADISON

On February 24, 1803, in *Marbury* v. *Madison*, the U.S. Supreme Court ruled for the first time that an act of Congress was unconstitutional, thus establishing the doctrine of judicial review.

The Supreme Court's growing conflict with President Thomas Jefferson and the Republican Congress came to a head after Secretary of State James Madison, on Jefferson's orders, withheld from William Marbury the commission of his appointment (March 2, 1801), by former President John Adams, as justice of the peace in the District of Columbia. Marbury—one of the so-called midnight appointments made in the final hours of Adams's term under the Judiciary Act of 1801—requested the Supreme Court to issue a writ of mandamus compelling Madison to deliver his commission. In denying his request, the Court held that it lacked jurisdiction because Section 13 of the Judiciary Act passed by Congress in 1789, which authorized the Court to issue such a writ, was unconstitutional and thus invalid. Chief Justice Marshall declared that in any such conflict between the Constitution and a law passed by Congress, the Constitution must always take precedence. The apparent "victory" for Jefferson was in fact a landmark in asserting the power of the Supreme Court's life-tenured justices, which Jefferson hated and feared.

can sometimes frustrate efforts to obtain pronouncements on disputed issues.

Although the U.S. courts are the guardians of the Constitution, they are not bound to consider all the provisions of the Constitution justiciable. Under the doctrine of political questions, the Supreme Court has refused at times to apply standards prescribed by or deducible from the Constitution to issues that it believed could be better decided by the political branches of government. Since *Luther* v. *Borden* (1849), for example, it is a matter of settled practice that the court will not use Article IV, Section 4—which provides that the states must have a republican form of government—to invalidate state laws; it is for Congress and the president to decide whether a particular state government is republican in form. Many military and foreign policy questions, such as the constitutionality of a particular war, likewise have been considered political and therefore non-justiciable.

On the other hand, the political-question doctrine has not prevented the Supreme Court from asserting its jurisdiction in cases that are politically sensitive. Thus, in *United States* v. *Nixon* (1974), the court ruled that President Richard Nixon was required to turn over to federal authorities the tape recordings that confirmed his complicity in the Watergate scandal. The doctrine also did not prevent the court from intervening in the presidential election of 2000, when it halted the recount of ballots in the disputed state of Florida and effectively confirmed George W.

The chairman of the Palm Beach County canvassing board continues the manual recount of 800 to 1,000 disputed ballots past deadline during the presidential election of 2000.

Bush's victory, despite forceful arguments that, under the Constitution and relevant federal statutes, the matter was clearly one for Florida and Congress to decide.

THE FOUR PILLARS OF REVIEW

Judicial review is designed to be more impartial than review by other institutions of government. This does not mean, however, that it is immune to policy considerations or to changes in the needs and political attitudes of the people. As a matter of fact, the Supreme Court's reading of the Constitution has itself evolved in the course of more than two centuries, in accordance with the large transformations that have occurred in American society. Given the structure of the U.S. Constitution, the Supreme Court historically has resolved constitutional disputes in four main areas: the relations between the states and the national government, the separation of powers within the national government, the right of government to regulate the economy, and individual rights and freedoms. In each of these areas the court's conception of the Constitution has undergone substantial changes.

From 1789 through the Civil War era, the Supreme Court was a crucial participant in nation building, its decisions reinforcing the newly born structures of the federal system. The court's rulings established judicial supremacy in constitutional interpretation, gave force to the national supremacy clause of Article VI of the Constitution—which declared the Constitution the supreme law of the United States—and laid the foundation for the power of the federal government to intervene in the national economy by broadly interpreting its constitutional power to regulate interstate commerce. In contrast, during the decades of industrialization and economic growth that followed the Civil War, the court was skeptical of attempts at economic regulation by the federal government. Until the Great Depression spawned the New Deal legislation of President Franklin D. Roosevelt, the court ruled that areas of economic activity were matters for state legislation or not subject to government regulation at all.

Until the New Deal, the court used the provisions of the Constitution concerning individual rights and freedoms primarily to protect property and economic liberties against state and federal efforts to interfere with the market. Thus, it often used the due process clause of the Fifth and Fourteenth amendments (no person shall be deprived of "life, liberty, or property, without due process of law") to invalidate social legislation, such as laws establishing minimum or maximum working hours. In contrast, the court's agenda was subsequently dominated by litigation directly raising questions involving civil and political rights and freedoms, as well as individual equality before the law. Due process claims focused primarily on procedural rights in criminal and administrative areas.

APPLICATIONS OF JUDICIAL REVIEW

The consequences of judicial review in the United States have been enormous. From the late 1930s through the 1960s, a liberal Supreme Court used its powers of judicial review to broaden democratic participation in government and to expand the rights of citizens, especially those of minorities and the accused. Beginning in the 1970s, a more-conservative Supreme Court resisted the expansion of rights in many areas and limited the effects of previously established rights in others. Nevertheless, it did not, by and large, overturn the panoply of rights created by its predecessor.

A few examples may illustrate the differences that have developed in the past century between American and European applications of judicial review. In the area of freedom of expression, the American doctrine holds that no seditious or subversive speech can be punished unless it poses a "clear and present danger" of inciting immediate unlawful action. The freedom to express unorthodox opinions is also recognized by European constitutions and upheld by the constitutional courts, but European doctrine has not accepted the American standard of clear and present danger or prior restraint. The Federal Constitutional Court of Germany has dissolved neo-Nazi and other parties on the basis of constitutional provisions without even considering the element of actual "danger." In the United States, the law of libel concerning public figures actively protects free speech. Under the doctrine of *New York Times* v. *Sullivan* (1964), plaintiffs who are public figures cannot win unless they prove that the libeler knowingly asserted a false statement.

The separation of church and state, as provided for by the First Amendment to the U.S. Constitution, has led the U.S. Supreme Court to rule in a series of cases that officially sanctioned

In the mid-20th century, during a period of expansion of individual rights, the U.S. Supreme Court declared racial segregation in schools unconstitutional (*Brown* v. *Board of Education of Topeka*, 1954).

Bible reading, prayer, and religious instruction in public schools as unconstitutional. Separation of church and state, although contemplated in principle by European constitutions, is sometimes tempered by agreements between church and state. Thus, no European court has ruled that accords giving students the opportunity to attend religious courses in public schools violate the principle of religious freedom or the principle of the equality of all citizens before the law.

For the most part, European courts have not

In Washington, D.C., on June 17, 1963, the Supreme Court ruled 8–1 in *School District of Abington Township* v. *Schempp* that it is unconstitutional for a state to require Bible reading and recitation of the Lord's Prayer in public schools. Madalyn Murray had challenged a Baltimore City school board regulation in a case that was consolidated with *Schempp*.

openly defied the political powers of the state in the way of the U.S. Supreme Court. Even when European courts have challenged such powers by annulling laws that were supposedly of special interest, the conflict has not been serious. The greater prudence of European courts is partly due to the fact that their status as independent and active agencies is relatively recent, while the tradition of judicial review in the United States is firmly rooted.

CHAPTER THREE

FUNCTIONS OF COURTS

The primary function of any court system is to help keep domestic peace. If there were no institution that was accepted by the citizens of a society as an impartial and authoritative judge of whether a person had committed a crime and, if so, what type of punishment should be meted out, vigilantes offended by the person's conduct might well take the law into their own hands and proceed to punish the alleged miscreant according to their uncontrolled discretion. If no agency were empowered to decide private disputes impartially and authoritatively, people would have to settle their disputes by themselves, with power rather than legitimate authority likely being the basis of such decisions.

DECIDING DISPUTES

In the course of helping to keep the peace, courts are called upon to decide controversies. If, in a criminal case, the defendant denies committing the acts charged against him, the court must choose between his version of the facts and that presented by the prosecution. If the defendant asserts that his actions did not constitute criminal behaviour, the court (often aided by a jury) must decide whether his view of the law and facts or the prosecution's is correct. In a civil case, if the defendant disputes the plaintiff's account of what happened between them—for example, whether they entered into a certain contract or agreement—or if he disputes the plaintiff's view of the legal significance of whatever occurred—for example, whether the agreement was legally binding—the court again must choose between the contentions of the parties. The issues presented to, and decided by, the court may be either factual, legal, or both.

Courts do not spend all their time resolving disputes between opposing parties. Many cases brought before the courts are not contested (e.g., a "no-fault" divorce or a routine debt-collection case). As no dispute exists over the facts or the law, the court's role in such cases is more administrative than adjudicatory. Most people arrested and

Unarmed teenager Trayvon Martin was killed in Florida on February 26, 2012, by neighborhood watch volunteer George Zimmerman. Zimmerman was acquitted of second-degree murder.

charged with a crime, however, plead guilty. If they do so with full understanding and without any coercion, the judge generally accepts their admission of guilt. Then, the sole question for the court is to decide whether the defendant should go to jail, pay a fine, pay restitution to the victim, and/or be subjected to other corrective treatment. The vast majority of civil cases are also uncontested, or at least settled prior to trial; in some instances, serious negotiations begin only after a lawsuit has been filed. In many Western countries, these suits are settled by the parties themselves – without the intervention of the court.

Since the late 20th century there has been a decreased reliance upon trials to settle disputes. The decline in court usage reflects several legal and social trends, most notably the increased desire of the parties to seek immediate relief and the increased options in the systems available to do just that. In the United States, for example, most divorce cases are uncontested, both parties usually being eager to terminate the marriage and often agreeing on related questions concerning support and the custody of children. All the court does in such cases is review what the parties have agreed upon and give the agreement official approval and the legitimacy of law. In other instances, disputes are settled through alternative dispute resolution such as arbitration, in which the parties agree that the decision will carry the full, binding force of law. Arbitration is commonly used in commercial and labor disputes.

Many civil cases are settled outside of court in an office or conference room between the two opposing parties and their lawyers, without the involvement of a judge or jury.

Many other uncontested matters come before courts, such as the adoption of children, the distribution of assets in trusts and estates, and the establishment of corporations. Occasionally, questions of law or fact arise that have to be decided by the court, but normally all that is required is judicial supervision and approval. Thus, much of what courts do is administrative in nature.

JUDICIAL LAWMAKING

All courts apply statutes formulated by legislative bodies, though procedures vary greatly between common-law and civil-law countries. In applying these rules, courts must also interpret them by transforming them from generalities to specifics and filling gaps left unaddressed by lawmakers when the legislation was first drafted. As courts decide disputes in individual cases, they create an important by-product: rules for deciding future cases. In common-law systems, such decisions are called "precedents"—rules and policies with just as much authority as a law passed by a legislature.

The common-law system of creating precedents is sometimes called stare decisis (literally, "to stand by decided matters"). Judges are expected to follow earlier decisions, because the goal of the law is to render uniform and predictable justice. Fairness demands that if one individual is dealt with in a certain way today, then another, future individual engaging in substantially identical conduct under substantially identical conditions should be dealt with in the same way. This system of stare decisis is sometimes referred to as "judge-made law," as the precedent is set by a judge, not legislature. In civil-law countries, all judicial decisions are, in theory, based upon legislative enactments, and the doctrine of judicial precedent does not apply. Judges merely "apply" the law created by the legislature. Practice often departs from this theory, with gaps in legislation filled by judicial decisions. These decisions are then published in legal volumes and relied upon by lawyers and judges. While they are not considered binding in the sense that judges are legally obliged to follow earlier decisions, neither are they forgotten or disregarded. In actual practice, they have almost as much influence as statutory interpretations in countries that formally adhere to the doctrine of stare decisis.

Judicial lawmaking is more pervasive and more frankly acknowledged in common-law countries than in civil-law ones. Whenever judges are confronted with a dispute for which there is no clear statutory answer—and this occurs with considerable regularity— they must render decisions in accordance with their own conceptions of justice. The total accumulation of all these judicial decisions is what constitutes "the common law"—the consequence of judges deciding cases and setting forth their reasons. Large areas of conduct are governed solely by judge-made law. To speak of precedent as "binding" even in common-law systems is somewhat misleading.

Even more significant, earlier decisions can be over-ruled by the courts that rendered them when the judges conclude that the decisions were so erroneous or unwise that they are unsuited for current or future application. The Supreme Court of the United States, for example, has overruled many of its own earlier decisions. Many of these reversals have been in the field of constitutional law, in which simple legislative correction of an erroneous judicial interpretation of the Constitution is impossible and in which the only alternative is constitutional amendment. The power to overrule decisions extends to areas of purely statutory and purely judge-made law as well, areas in which

Lord Speaker Norman Fowler addresses the House of Lords, in session in its chamber at the House of Parliament, London, September 5, 2016.

legislative action would be equally capable of accomplishing needed changes. Even in the United Kingdom, which does not have a codified constitution and which has traditionally followed a far more rigid doctrine of stare decisis than the United States, the Supreme Court, in its role as the highest court, sometimes departs from precedent.

REVIEW OF ADMINISTRATIVE DECISIONS

Administrative agencies of various kinds (e.g., the Food and Drug Administration in the United States) exist alongside the courts in nearly every country. Some do substantially the same kind of work as is done by courts in substantially the same manner; others, however, have

LAWMAKING IN THE LOWER COURTS

All lower courts in the United States also possess and exercise the same powers as the Supreme Court. Whenever a question arises in any U.S. court at any level as to the constitutionality of a statute or executive action, that court is obligated to determine its validity in the course of deciding the case before it. Indeed, the case may have been brought for the sole and express purpose of testing the constitutionality of the statute (e.g., a law requiring racial segregation or restricting freedom of speech), or it may be an

A judicial circuit court such as this one in downtown Tampa, Florida, has the same powers as the Supreme Court, though the decisions made in the circuit court can be appealed and subjected to review by the Supreme Court.

ordinary civil or criminal case in which a constitutional question incidental to the main purpose of the proceeding is raised (e.g., the legality of a search and seizure by the authorities). Every judge in the United States is legally empowered to engage in constitutional interpretation. When a lower court decides a constitutional question, however, its decision is subject to appellate review, sometimes at more than one level. When a state statute is challenged as violating the state constitution, the final authority is the supreme court of that state; when a federal or state statute or a state constitutional provision is challenged as violating the Constitution of the United States, the ultimate arbiter is the U.S. Supreme Court.

different functions (e.g., the issuing of licenses and the payment of social-welfare benefits).

The relationship between such agencies and regular courts differs between common-law and civil-law countries. In common-law countries, the actions of administrative agencies are subject to review in the ordinary courts. If the agency decides controversies in substantially the same manner as a court but in a different and more limited area, judicial control takes much the same form of appellate review as is provided for the decisions of lower courts. The objective of reviewing the record of the proceedings is to determine whether the administrative agency acted within the scope of its jurisdiction, whether there was any evidence to support its conclusion, whether procedures were fair, and whether the governing law was correctly interpreted and applied.

Administrative decisions are seldom upset by the courts, because most judges believe that administrative agencies have expertise in their area of specialization. However, the agencies can be and occasionally are overruled, which reflects the large degree of judicial control over other agencies of government that characterizes common-law systems. If the administrative agency does not engage in formal adjudication, it produces no record of its proceedings for judicial review. Nevertheless, the agency's decisions can be challenged in court by way of trial rather

Then-commissioner of the Food and Drug Administration (FDA) Margaret Hamburg (2009–15) speaks during a daily briefing at the White House in 2011.

than appeal. The same problems are presented for judicial determination: did the agency act within its jurisdiction, did it correctly follow the law, and was there any rational or factual basis for its action?

In many civil-law countries, the ordinary courts have no control over administrative agencies. Their decisions are reviewed by a special tribunal that is engaged exclusively in that work and has nothing to do with cases of the type that come into the courts. Its function is solely appellate and is limited to specialized areas entrusted to the administrative agencies. The prototype of this type of tribunal is France's Conseil d'État, which decides and advises on issues put to it by the president, cabinet, or parliament. Such tribunals also have been established in Belgium, Egypt, Greece, Spain, and Turkey.

ENFORCEMENT OF JUDICIAL DECISIONS

The method of enforcing a judicial decision depends upon its nature. If it does nothing more than declare legal rights, as is true of a simple divorce decree (merely severing marital ties, not awarding alimony or the custody of children) or a declaratory judgment (e.g., interpreting a contract or a statute), no enforcement is needed. If a judgment orders a party to do or to refrain from doing a certain act, as happens when an injunction is issued, the court itself takes the first step in enforcing the judgment by holding in contempt anyone who refuses to obey its order and sentencing him to pay a fine or to go to jail. Thereafter, enforcement is in the hands of the executive branch of government, acting through its law-enforcement and correctional authorities.

As a member of the executive branch in the United States, the role of the sheriff is varied but involves enforcing the decisions made by the judiciary branch.

In routine criminal cases and in civil cases that result in the award of monetary damages, courts have little to do with the enforcement of their judgments. Instead, this is the function of the executive branch of government, acting through sheriffs, marshals, jailers, and similar officials.

Some judgments issued by courts are extremely controversial and encounter intense public opposition (e.g., the decision of the Supreme Court of the United States ordering racial desegregation of the public schools in 1954). When voluntary compliance with such a judgment is refused, forcible methods of enforcement are necessary, sometimes extending to the deployment of armed forces under the control of the executive branch. The withdrawal of executive support seldom occurs, even when decisions are directed against the executive branch itself. When such executive support is withheld, however, the courts are rendered impotent.

CHAPTER FOUR

TYPES OF COURTS

There are many different types of courts and many ways to classify and describe them. Basic distinctions must be made between criminal and civil courts, between courts of general jurisdiction and those of limited jurisdiction, and between appellate and trial courts.

CRIMINAL COURTS

Criminal courts deal with persons accused of committing a crime: deciding whether they are guilty and, if so, determining the consequences they shall suffer. The prosecution of alleged offenders is generally pursued in the name of the public (e.g., *The People* v. ...), because crimes are considered offenses against society at large. The public is represented by an official such as a district attorney (prosecutor), procurator, or police officer. Courts are neutral in criminal proceedings, favouring neither the prosecution nor the defense. The impartiality of the court is reinforced where juries are used to decide the guilt or innocence of the defendant.

The role of the criminal court in civil-law systems is quite different from its role in common-law ones. Civil-law countries assign a more active role to the judge and a more passive role to counsel. Instead of being passive recipients of evidence, judges in civil-law systems often direct the presentation of evidence and even order that certain evidence be produced. Thus, procedure in civil-law systems is considered inquisitorial. Judges in this system have an independent responsibility to discover the facts. In the common-law courts, adversary procedures prevail; the lawyers for both sides bear responsibility for producing evidence and do most of the questioning of witnesses. Advocates of the adversarial system hold that a just outcome is most likely to result when all possible relevant information is placed before an impartial adjudicator (the judge or the jury). Self-interest motivates both the defense and the prosecution to provide all possible evidence relevant to its side of the case. Where the jury system is used, the jury is supposed to constitute an unbiased sample of people predisposed to favouring neither the defense nor the prosecution, and the judge serves as a "legal referee" who ensures that proper procedures are followed (e.g., barring the introduction of illegally obtained evidence or other information deemed inadmissible). The adversarial system, and its associated conception of justice, is a pillar of the common-law tradition, as evidenced in the U.S., British, and Canadian systems of criminal justice.

If a defendant is found guilty, he is sentenced, again according to law and within limits predetermined by legislation. The most common sentences are fines, short terms of imprisonment, and probation (which allows the offender freedom under state supervision). Extremely serious cases may call for a long term of imprisonment (e.g., life in prison) or (in some countries) even capital punishment. During the last third of the 20th century, the death penalty began to disappear from many criminal codes throughout the world; it remains in effect in the United States, Iran, China, and several other countries.

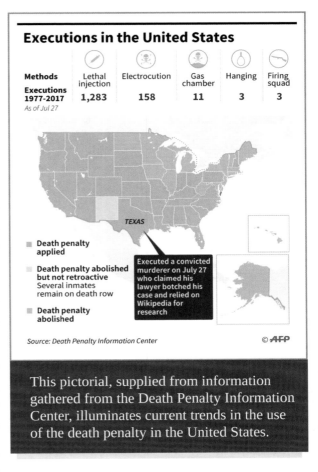

Executions in the United States

Methods	Lethal injection	Electrocution	Gas chamber	Hanging	Firing squad
Executions 1977-2017 As of Jul 27	1,283	158	11	3	3

TEXAS

■ Death penalty applied

Death penalty abolished but not retroactive Several inmates remain on death row

■ Death penalty abolished

Executed a convicted murderer on July 27 who claimed his lawyer botched his case and relied on Wikipedia for research

Source: Death Penalty Information Center © AFP

This pictorial, supplied from information gathered from the Death Penalty Information Center, illuminates current trends in the use of the death penalty in the United States.

CIVIL COURTS

Civil courts deal with "private" controversies, particularly disputes between individuals, private businesses, or institutions (e.g., a disagreement over the terms of a contract or the cause of an automobile accident). The public is not ordinarily a party to the litigation, for its interest is limited to providing just and acceptable rules in a forum where the dispute can be impartially and peacefully resolved. These factors are important because the use of the civil courts is voluntary.

The government may be involved in civil litigation if it stands in the same relation to a private party as another individual might stand. If a government postal truck hits a pedestrian, for example, the government might be sued civilly by the injured person; or if the government contracted to purchase supplies that turned out to be defective, it might sue the dealer for damages in a civil court. In such proceedings, the government acts as a private party.

The objective of a civil action is not explicitly punishment or correction of the defendant or the setting of an example but rather restoration of the parties to the positions they would have occupied had no legal wrong been committed. The most common civil remedy is a judgment for monetary damages; others include injunctions ordering the defendant to do—or to refrain from doing—a certain act or judgments restoring property to its rightful owner. For example, a celebrity might obtain an injunction against a stalker, requiring that the person not come within a certain distance of the celebrity at any time.

A single incident may give rise to both civil liability and criminal prosecution. In some countries (e.g., France), both types of responsibility can be determined in a single proceeding under a concept known as adhesion, but in common-law countries, there is no such procedure. Two separate actions must be brought independent of each other. For example, in the United States in the mid-1990s, former football star O.J. Simpson was tried in a California criminal court on a charge of having murdered his ex-wife and her friend; although he was acquitted in that litigation (in which a guilty verdict required proof "beyond a reasonable doubt"), in a subsequent civil suit (in which a guilty verdict required proof by a "preponderance of the evidence"), he was found liable and was ordered to pay restitution to the families of the victims. In the United

This famous photograph shows O.J. Simpson attempting to exonerate himself while on trial in June 1995 by demonstrating that his hands don't fit the gloves found at the scene of the crimes.

States, such collateral civil lawsuits have become attractive to victims of alleged crimes, particularly because the standard of proof in civil courts is dramatically lower than it is in criminal courts.

COURTS OF GENERAL OR LIMITED JURISDICTION

Although there are some courts that handle only criminal cases and others that deal with only civil cases, a more common pattern is for a single court to be vested with both civil and criminal jurisdiction. Examples of such courts include the High Court of Justice for England and Wales and many of the trial courts found in the United States of America. These are called courts of general jurisdiction, which signifies that they can handle almost any type of controversy, though they may not have jurisdiction over certain types of specialized cases, such as immigration. Such courts are also described as superior courts, because they handle serious criminal cases as well as important civil cases. Most high appellate courts (e.g., the U.S. Supreme Court) are courts of general jurisdiction, hearing both civil and criminal appeals. Even if a court possesses general or very broad jurisdiction, it may be organized into specialized branches: criminal cases; civil cases; juvenile cases; and so forth. This way, judges can be transferred from one type of work to another and cases instituted in the wrong branch will still be heard.

There are many kinds of specialized courts: probate courts deal with the administration of the estates of deceased persons; commercial courts deal with disputes between merchants; traffic courts process motor vehicle offenses such as speeding and improper parking; and labor courts deal with disputes between employers and employees. Although these courts are of limited jurisdiction, they may exercise substantial power.

Juvenile courts deal with misconduct by children and the neglect or maltreatment of children. The procedures of juvenile courts are more informal than adult criminal courts, and the facilities available for the pretrial detention of children and their incarceration, if necessary, after trial are different. American attitudes are bifurcated on the subject of juvenile law; when minors are victims or can potentially be victimized, law and society typically agree that the purpose of the law is to protect the innocent. This is evident in laws designed to protect minors from exposure to obscene material and sexual predators and in divorce and custody law. When minors commit a violent act, public and political sentiments often change; the minor is no longer seen as innocent and deserving of the protection of the law. While some may seek to rehabilitate the youth and desire lenient punishment, others consider a youth of any age who commits a crime as mature enough to be sentenced accordingly.

In most jurisdictions, there are institutions called inferior courts. These are often staffed by part-time judges who are not necessarily trained in the law. They handle

DISTRICT COURTS

The district courts of the United States, formally called the United States District Courts, consist of the basic trial-level courts of the federal judicial system. The courts, which exercise both criminal and civil jurisdiction, are based in the 94 judicial districts throughout the United States. Each state has at least one judicial district, as do the District of Columbia, Puerto Rico, the Virgin Islands, Guam, and the Northern Mariana Islands. A populous state may have as many as four districts.

As required by Article III of the Constitution of the United States, the judges of district courts are nominated by the president and confirmed by the Senate and hold their offices "during good Behaviour [sic]." Magistrate judges, who are appointed by federal district judges on a full-time basis for eight-year terms or on a part-time basis for four-year terms, play an increasingly important role in assisting district judges. Indeed, with the consent of the parties to the case, they may conduct trials and enter decisions themselves. Decisions of the district courts are normally subject to appeal, typically to the United States Court of Appeals for the region in which the district court is located.

minor civil cases involving small sums of money, such as bill collections, and minor criminal cases carrying light penalties. Such courts may also handle the early phases of more serious criminal cases—including fixing bail, advising defendants of their rights, appointing counsel, and conducting preliminary hearings to determine whether the evidence is sufficient to justify holding defendants for trial in higher superior courts.

APPELLATE COURTS

Appellate courts are positioned above the trial courts to review their work and correct any errors that may have occurred. They usually consist of several judges. The jurisdiction of the appellate courts is often general, handling both criminal appeals and civil appeals. Because appellate review usually must be sought by a party aggrieved by the judgment in the trial court, there are far fewer appeals than trials and even fewer second appeals. The principle of due process creates a right to at least one review by a higher court, so intermediate appeals courts are typically obliged to hear the cases appealed to them. High courts—many state supreme courts and the U.S. Supreme Court—are not obliged to hear any particular case, and may issue decisions in only a tiny fraction of the cases appealed to them.

There are three basic types of appellate review. The first is retrial of the case, with the appellate court hearing evidence and proceeding in much the same manner as the initial court. This trial de novo is used when the first trial was conducted by an inferior court. The second type of review is based in part on a dossier, or record of all evidence and findings. The reviewing court has the power to hear the same witnesses again and take additional evidence, but often relies on the record already made. This is used in civil-law countries for the first stage of appellate review even when the original trial was conducted in a superior court. The third type of review is based on a written record of proceedings. The reviewing court uses the record to determine whether errors were committed requiring reversal or modification of the judgment or a new trial altogether. The emphasis is on questions of law, not questions of fact. This type of review prevails both in civil- and common-law countries. The highest appellate court rulings also become guidelines for future cases.

The United States Courts of Appeals con-

A court official emerges from a federal appeals court after it ruled against lifting the stay on President Donald Trump's executive order imposing a temporary immigration ban on seven Muslim-majority nations in San Francisco, California, on February 9, 2017.

sist of thirteen intermediate appellate courts within the federal judicial system: twelve courts whose jurisdictions are geographically apportioned, plus the United States Court of Appeals for the Federal Circuit. Each regional court can review all final decisions and certain interlocutory (provisional) decisions of district courts within its jurisdiction, except those appealable only to the Supreme Court of the United States. A court of appeals can also review and enforce orders of federal regulatory agencies, such as the Federal Trade Commission and the National Labor Relations Board. They typically sit in panels of three judges, and cases are decided by majority vote. All decisions of the courts of appeals are subject to discretionary review or appeal in the Supreme Court. The Court of Appeals for the Federal Circuit hears appeals from U.S. district and territorial courts in patent and trademark cases and cases in which the United States or one of its agencies is a defendant.

CHAPTER FIVE

THE SUPREME COURT OF THE UNITED STATES

The Supreme Court of the United States is the final court of appeal and final expositor of the Constitution of the United States. Within the framework of litigation, the Supreme Court marks the boundaries of authority between state and nation, state and state, and government and citizen.

SCOPE AND JURISDICTION

The Supreme Court was created by the Constitutional Convention of 1787 as the head of a federal court system, though it was not formally established until Congress passed the Judiciary Act in 1789. Although the Constitution outlined the powers, structure, and functions of the legislative and executive branches of government in some detail, it did not do the same for the judicial branch, leaving much of that responsibility to Congress and stipulating only that judicial power be "vested in one supreme Court, and in such inferior Courts as the Congress may from time to time ordain and establish." As the country's court of last resort, the Supreme Court is an appellate body, vested with the authority to act in cases arising under the Constitution, laws, or treaties of the United States; in controversies to which the United States is a party; in disputes between states or between citizens of different states; and in cases of admiralty and maritime jurisdiction. In suits affecting ambassadors, other public ministers, and consuls and in cases in which states are a party, the Supreme Court has original jurisdiction—i.e., it serves as a trial court. Relatively few cases reach the court through its original jurisdiction, however; instead, the vast majority of the court's business and nearly all of its most influential decisions derive from its appellate jurisdiction.

Thirty-nine members of the Constitutional Convention signed the U.S. Constitution on September 17, 1787. While the Supreme Court was created there, it was not formalized until Congress passed the Judiciary Act in 1789.

SIZE, MEMBERSHIP, AND ORGANIZATION

The organization of the federal judicial system, including the size of the Supreme Court, is established by Congress. From 1789 to 1807 the court comprised six justices. In 1807 a seventh justice was added, followed by an eighth and a ninth in 1837 and a tenth in 1863. Since 1869, the number of justices has been set at nine. The size of the court has sometimes been subject to political manipulation; for example, in the 1860s Congress reduced the number of justices to eight to ensure that President Andrew Johnson, whom the House of Representatives had impeached and the Senate only narrowly acquitted, could not appoint a new justice to the court; and in the 1930s President Franklin D. Roosevelt asked Congress to consider legislation (which it rejected) that would have allowed the president to appoint an additional justice for each member of the court aged seventy years or older who refused to retire.

According to the Constitution, appointments to the Supreme Court and to the lower federal courts are made by the president with the advice and consent of the Senate, though presidents have rarely consulted the Senate before making a nomination. The Senate Judiciary Committee ordinarily conducts hearings on nominations to the Supreme Court, and a simple majority of the full Senate is required for confirmation. When the position of chief justice is vacant, the president may appoint a chief justice from outside the court or elevate an associate justice to the position. In either case a simple majority of the Senate must approve the appointment. Members of the Supreme Court are appointed for life terms, though they may be expelled if they are impeached by the House of Representatives and convicted in the Senate. Only one justice has been impeached, Samuel Chase, who was acquitted in 1805. In 1969 Abe Fortas resigned under threat of impeachment for alleged financial improprieties unrelated to his duties on the court.

The federal judicial system originally comprised only trial courts of original jurisdiction and the Supreme Court. As the country grew in size, and in the absence of intermediate appellate courts, the volume of cases awaiting review increased, and fidelity to Supreme Court precedents varied significantly among the lower courts. To remedy this problem, Congress passed the Circuit Court of Appeals Act (1891), which established nine intermediate courts with final authority over appeals from federal district courts, except when the case in question was of exceptional public importance. The Judiciary Act of 1925 (popularly known

Associate Justice Samuel Chase was impeached, then acquitted, in 1805.

as the Judges' Bill), which was sponsored by the court itself, carried the reforms farther, greatly limiting obligatory jurisdiction (which required the Supreme Court to review a case) and expanding the classes of cases that the court could accept at its own discretion through the issue of a writ of certiorari. Further changes were enacted in 1988, when Congress passed legislation that required the Supreme Court to hear appeals of cases involving legislative reapportionment and federal civil rights and antitrust laws. Currently, there are twelve geographic judicial circuits and a court of appeals for the federal circuit, located in Washington, D.C. Roughly 98 percent of federal cases end with a decision by one of the lower appellate courts.

PROCEDURES AND POWER

The term of the Supreme Court begins by statute on the first Monday in October and typically ends in late June. Each year the court receives thousands of certiorari requests. The number of these requests has increased dramatically since World War II—a reflection of the country's population growth, a progressively more litigious legal culture, and a surge in the demands placed by citizens on government.

All certiorari requests are circulated among the justices. The chief justice leads the court in developing a "discuss list" of potential cases, though the associate justices may request that additional cases be placed on the list. By the so-called Rule of Four, apparently developed in the late 19th century, the decision to grant certiorari requires the assent of at least four justices. Once the decision to hear a case has been made, lower-court records and briefs are delivered to the court and oral arguments are scheduled. Interested third parties also may submit their opinions to the court by filing an amicus curiae (Latin: "friend of the court") brief. With rare exceptions, the petitioners and respondents are each allotted 30 minutes of time to present their arguments to the court. The justices hear neither witnesses nor evidence. Each side in the case attempts to persuade the justices that the Constitution should be interpreted in a manner that supports its point of view.

The decision-making process involves two major judgments. First, in a vote that is usually kept secret, the justices decide the merits of the case; then they issue the official written decision of the court. The first judgment determines who will write the official decision. By tradition, if the chief justice is in the majority, he selects which justice will author the court's verdict. If he is in the minority, the longest-serving member of the majority makes the decision-writing appointment. Since the era of John Marshall, chief justice from 1801 to 1835, it has been common practice for the court to issue formal opinions to justify its decisions, though the Constitution does not require it to do so. Drafts of all opinions circulate among the justices, and all justices may concur with or dissent from any decision, in full or in part. The final decision effectively represents

SELF-INCRIMINATION AND THE MIRANDA WARNING

Controversy has surrounded Supreme Court decisions on the issue of self-incrimination—the giving of evidence that might expose a person to punishment for a crime. In the United States' judicial system, a person other than the accused cannot refuse to testify; he may cite his privilege against self-incrimination, after which the judge decides whether he must testify. If required, he must answer all questions except those he considers to be self-incriminating.

In the pivotal *Miranda* v. *Arizona* case (1966), the U.S. Supreme Court reversed an Arizona court's conviction of Ernesto Miranda on charges of kidnapping and rape, creating a code of conduct for police interrogations of criminal suspects held in custody. After being identified in a police lineup, Miranda had been questioned by police; he confessed and signed a written statement without first being told that he had the right to have a lawyer present to advise him or that he had the right to remain silent. This confession was used in his initial trial to obtain conviction. Chief Justice Earl Warren, writing for the 5–4 majority of the justices, declared that the prosecution may not use statements made by a person under questioning in police custody unless certain minimum procedural safeguards are followed to ensure "that the individual is accorded his privilege under the Fifth Amendment" against self-incrimination. These include informing arrested persons that they have the right to remain silent, that anything they say may be used against them as evidence, and that they have the right to the counsel of an attorney.

The *Miranda* ruling shocked the law-enforcement community. Critics said that the court, in seeking to protect the rights of individuals, had seriously weakened law enforcement agencies. Several later decisions limited the scope of the *Miranda* safeguards. In *Salinas* v. *Texas* (2013), the court ruled that someone brought in for police questioning must state that he is invoking his Fifth Amendment right to remain silent. Otherwise, prosecutors may use his refusal to answer a question as evidence against him during trial.

the supreme law of the land and is expected to be used as controlling constitutional doctrine by lower courts.

The Supreme Court's power of judicial review enables it to declare acts of Congress or the state legislatures unconstitutional. Executive, administrative, and judicial actions also are subject to review by the court. Because judicial review is not explicitly mentioned in the Constitution, some critics have charged that the framers did not intend for the court to exercise such power. Nevertheless, since the late 19th century the vast majority of legal scholars have accepted judicial review as a proper power of the court.

HISTORICAL TRENDS

Any assessment of the unifying forces in American society must ascribe a significant role to the Supreme Court. In its institutional infancy, the court necessarily addressed structural and functional questions involving, among other issues, federalism, express and implied powers, checks and balances, and the separation of powers. During the mid- to late 19th century, the court employed the Constitution's commerce clause (Article I Section 8) to nullify state laws of taxation or regulation that discriminated against or unduly burdened interstate commerce. The clause subsequently was used to uphold the power of Congress to regulate vast sectors of the economy.

Whereas the commerce clause has been the chief doctrinal source of federal power over the economy, the due-process clause of the Fifth Amendment and the equal-protection clause of the Fourteenth Amendment have been the principal sources of protection of persons and corporations against arbitrary or repressive acts of government. These clauses were used at first to protect property rights, but in the 1920s they began to be applied to civil liberties, particularly in the extension of Bill of Rights guarantees to state actions.

By the middle of the century, the equal-protection clause, which had been designed to protect the rights of emancipated slaves, was being used to strike down laws that were racially discriminatory, and all rights guaranteed by the First Amendment had been "incorporated" (made applicable to the states) through the due-process clause of the Fourteenth Amendment. By the end of the 20th century, the court found itself addressing issues that had previously been considered off-limits according to the political-question doctrine, which it had invoked to avoid entering into questions that it thought were best decided by legislatures (e.g., prison administration, the operation of districting systems, the 2000 presidential election, and marriage rights). While broadening the concept of justiciable disputes, the court also sought to limit congressional power to control the affairs of the states. In a variety of cases concerning issues such as state immunity from lawsuits, commerce, and criminal procedure, a states' rights approach was adopted by the court's conservative majority.

The opinions of the Supreme Court, including the dissenting opinions of individual justices, often have been considered epitomes of legal reasoning. Through these opinions, the court serves to clarify, refine, and test the philosophical ideals written into the Constitution and to translate them into working principles for a federal union under law. Beyond its specific contributions, this symbolic and pragmatic function may be regarded as the most significant role of the court.

CHAPTER SIX

CIVIL RIGHTS AND THE U.S. FEDERAL COURTS

Few efforts were made to change the South's institution of slavery until the first decades of the 19th century, when the country's territorial acquisitions in the West raised the question of which of the new territories would permit slavery and which would prohibit it. Sectional differences between the North and the South, centring on the issue of slavery, began to appear in the 1830s. When a bill introduced by Senator Stephen A. Douglas of Illinois opened up to slavery the huge territories of Kansas and Nebraska—land that had long been reserved for free states—Northerners began to organize into an antislavery political party called the Republican Party.

SLAVERY AND SECTIONAL CONFLICT

Beginning in 1855, Kansas became a field of battle between the free and the slave states, with disputes involving rival settlers and legislatures erupting into violence. A pro-slavery mob sacked the town of Lawrence, an antislavery stronghold, on May 21, 1856. In retaliation, free-state partisan John Brown led a small party in a raid upon pro-slavery settlers on Pottawatomie Creek on May 24–25, murdering five men as a warning to the slaveholders. On May 22 Preston S. Brooks, a South Carolina congressman, attacked Senator Charles Sumner of Massachusetts at his desk in the Senate chamber due to his support of Kansas abolitionists. In the 1856 presidential election, voting was polarized along sectional lines. Though James Buchanan, the Democratic nominee, was elected, John C. Frémont, the Republican candidate, received a majority of the votes in the free states.

Abolitionist John Brown was finally captured by U.S. Marines in the armory at Harpers Ferry, West Virginia, in 1859.

On March 6, 1857, in *Dred Scott* v. *John F.A. Sandford*, the Supreme Court made slavery legal in all the territories. Although the case was thought to have been unusual, several hundred suits for freedom were filed by or on behalf of slaves in the decades before the Civil War. In 1834, Dr. John Emerson took his slave, Dred Scott, with him from Missouri (a slave state) to Illinois (a free state) and finally into the Wisconsin Territory (a free territory under the provisions of the Missouri Compromise). After they returned to Missouri, where Dr. Emerson died in 1843, Dred Scott attempted to purchase his freedom from Emerson's widow. In 1846, with the help of antislavery lawyers, Dred Scott and his wife Harriett Robinson filed lawsuits in the Saint Louis Circuit Court on the grounds that their residence in a free state and a free territory had freed them. In 1850, the lower court declared Scott free, but the verdict was overturned in 1852 by the Missouri Supreme Court. Mrs. Emerson gave control of her late husband's estate to her brother, a resident of New York; as he was not subject to suit in Missouri, Scott's law-

Dred Scott.

yers filed a suit against him in the U.S. federal courts. The case eventually reached the U.S. Supreme Court, which announced its decision on March 6, 1857, two days after the inauguration of President James Buchanan.

As one of the seven justices denying Scott his freedom, Chief Justice Roger B. Taney declared that an African American could not be entitled to rights as a U.S. citizen. Taney went on to declare that the Missouri Compromise of 1820 was unconstitutional, because Congress had no power to prohibit slavery in the territories. Slaves were property, and masters were guaranteed their property rights under the Fifth Amendment—neither Congress nor a territorial legislature could deprive a citizen of his property without due process of law; only a state could exclude slavery. This decision marked the second time in the country's history that the Supreme Court declared an act of Congress unconstitutional. President Buchanan and the majority of the Supreme Court hoped the *Dred Scott* decision would mark the end of anti-slavery agitation. Instead, the decision increased antislavery sentiment in the North, strengthened the Republican Party, and fed the sectional antagonism that resulted in civil war in 1861.

RACIAL SEGREGATION AND DISCRIMINATION

Racial segregation is the practice of restricting people to certain areas of residence or separate institutions and facilities on the basis of race. Segregation provides a means of maintaining the economic advantages and superior social status of the politically dominant group. In the Southern states of the United States, legal segregation in public facilities lasted from the late 19th century into the 1950s. The Jim Crow system in the United States was built upon laws that enforced racial segregation in the South between the formal end of Reconstruction—the period (1865–77) after the American Civil War during which the former Confederate states were readmitted to the Union—and the beginning of a strong civil rights movement in the 1950s. From the late 1870s, Southern state legislatures passed laws

An African American man can be seen drinking at a water cooler for "colored" people at a streetcar terminal in Oklahoma City in 1939.

requiring the separation of whites from "persons of color" (anyone of ascertainable or suspected African ancestry) in public transportation and schools. The segregation principle was extended to parks, cemeteries, theatres, and restaurants in an effort to prevent contact between blacks and whites as equals. It was codified on local and state levels, most famously with the "separate but equal" decision of the U.S. Supreme Court in *Plessy* v. *Ferguson* (1896).

Louisiana shoemaker Homer Plessy, a light-skinned person of mixed race, was chosen by the Comité des Citoyens ("Citizens' Committee"), a group opposed to racial segregation in the South, to defy the segregation law that stipulated separate train cars for blacks and whites. Taking a seat in the whites-only car, Plessy informed the conductor that he was black and was arrested for his crime—hoping to have the "separate but equal" law proven unconstitutional in court. *Plessy* v. *Ferguson* was handed down by the U.S. Supreme Court on May 18, 1896. In an 8–1 majority decision, the court firmly advanced the controversial "separate but equal" doctrine for assessing the constitutionality of racial segregation laws. Decided nearly thirty years after the passage of the Fourteenth Amendment to the Constitution of the United States, which had granted full and equal citizenship rights to African Americans, the Plessy case was the first major inquiry into the meaning of the amendment's equal-protection clause. In upholding a Louisiana law that required the segregation of passengers on railroad cars, the court reasoned that equal protection is not violated as long as reasonably equal accommodations are provided to each racial group.

Despite a series of civil rights advances, the ruling remained a controlling judicial precedent until its reversal in the case of *Brown* v. *Board of Education of Topeka* (1954). Linda Brown, a third grader living in Topeka, Kansas, became the instrument of change: though she lived a few blocks from the local white elementary school, the seven-year-old had to walk a mile to attend the black elementary school. With the local NAACP, the Brown family filed suit. On May 17, 1954, the U.S. Supreme Court ruled unanimously that racial segregation in public schools violated the Fourteenth Amendment to the Constitution. The decision declared that separate educational facilities were inherently unequal. *Brown* v. *Board of Education of Topeka* effectively reversed the 1896 *Plessy* decision. Strictly speaking, the 1954 decision was limited to public schools, but it implied that segregation was not permissible in other public facilities.

CIVIL RIGHTS LEGISLATION OF THE 1960S

The civil rights movement, initiated by African Americans in the South in the 1950s and '60s, spurred the passage of the Civil Rights Act of 1964, which created provisions against discrimination based on race, color, religion, or national origin and segregation in voting, education, and the use of public facilities. Title I of the act guarantees equal voting rights by removing registration requirements and procedures biased against minorities and the under-privileged. Title II prohibits segregation or discrimination in places of public accommodation involved in interstate commerce. Title VII bans discrimination by trade unions, schools, or employers involved in interstate commerce or doing business with the federal government. It also applies to discrimination on the basis of sex, establishing a government agency, the Equal Employment Opportunity Commission (EEOC), to enforce these provisions. The act calls for the desegregation of public schools (Title IV), broadens the duties of the Civil Rights Commission (Title V), and assures nondiscrimination in the distribution of funds under federally assisted programs (Title VI). White anti-integration groups responded to the act with signifi-cant backlash in the form of protests, support for pro-seg-regation candidates for public office, and racial violence.

The constitutionality of the Civil Rights Act was immediately challenged in the test case *Heart of Atlanta Motel* v. *United States* (1964). After President Lyndon B. Johnson signed the Civil Rights Act on July 2, 1964, the owner of the Heart of Atlanta Motel in Georgia, who had previously refused to accept African American customers, filed suit, alleging that the prohibition of racial discrimi-nation contained in Title II of the Civil Rights Act rep-resented an invalid exercise of Congress's constitutional power to regulate interstate commerce. In a unanimous

Although President John F. Kennedy was unable to secure passage of the bill in Congress, a stronger version of the Civil Rights Act of 1964 was eventually passed with the urging of his successor, President Lyndon B. Johnson, who signed the bill into law following one of the longest debates in Senate history.

ruling issued on December 14, the Supreme Court ruled that in passing Title II, the U.S. Congress did not exceed the regulatory authority granted to it by the commerce clause of Article I of the U.S. Constitution. The motel was ordered to cease discriminating against African American customers.

In 1965, Congress passed the Voting Rights Act, which aimed to overcome legal barriers at the state and local levels that prevented African Americans from exercising their right to vote under the Fifteenth Amendment (1870) to the Constitution of the United States. Section 4 of the act set forth a formula for determining which jurisdictions were required (under Section 5 of the act) to seek federal approval of any proposed change to their electoral laws or procedures ("preclearance"). The formula identified as "covered jurisdictions" any state or political subdivision of a state that as of November 1964 imposed tests (such as literacy tests) or other devices as a condition of registration or of voting and was characterized by voter registration or voter turnout below 50 percent of the voting-age population. Although Sections 4 and 5 of the VRA were originally scheduled to expire after five years, they and other provisions of the act were renewed several times, including in 2006 for a period of 25 years.

In *Shelby County* v. *Holder* (2013), the Supreme Court declared (5–4) unconstitutional Section 4 of the Voting Rights Act. In its ruling, the court's majority noted that the coverage formula had been justified in 1965 by the fact that discriminatory voting practices and low voter registration and turnout were then pervasive in the jurisdictions it singled out, including nine mostly Southern states. Since that time, however, such problems had been almost completely eradicated, in large measure because of enforcement of the VRA itself. In light of current conditions, the

BUSING AND RACIAL INTEGRATION

Although the Supreme Court had struck down racial segregation in public schools through *Brown v. Board of Education of Topeka*, many schools remained segregated into the late 1960s. For example, in the mid-1960s, less than 5 percent of African American children attended integrated schools in Charlotte, North Carolina. Busing was used by white officials to maintain segregation, to the dissatisfaction of both black and white citizens. The NAACP, on behalf of Vera and Darius Swann, sued the Charlotte-Mecklenburg school district to allow their six-year-old son to attend the school closest to their home—one of Charlotte's few integrated schools. James McMillan, the federal district judge in the case, ruled in favour of the Swanns and oversaw the implementation of a busing strategy that integrated the district's schools. McMillan's decision was appealed to the U.S. Supreme Court, which upheld it in April 1971. The busing strategy was adopted elsewhere in the United States and played an instrumental role in integrating U.S. public schools.

The court subsequently placed limitations on *Swann* when it ruled in *Milliken* v. *Bradley* (1974) that mandatory busing across school district boundaries could be implemented only where it could be shown that districts had enacted policies that caused the original segregation. By the late 1980s and early 1990s, mandatory busing was slowly disappearing across the United States as a result of changing housing patterns, although a handful of school districts remained under such court orders. The legacy of busing remains controversial; while opponents argue that forced busing did little to change the racial makeup of most schools and school districts, proponents counter that such extreme measures were necessary to finally implement the reforms directed by *Brown*.

majority concluded, the coverage formula represented an unwarranted intrusion by the federal government on the covered states' power under the Tenth Amendment to regulate elections, as well as a violation of the "fundamental principle of equal sovereignty" among the states, which the court had recognized in *Northwest Austin Municipal Utility District No. One* v. *Holder* (2009). Notably, the court did not find fault with the VRA's Section 5 (which now became unenforceable) or with the notion of preclearance itself.

HISTORY OF AFFIRMATIVE ACTION

Affirmative action was initiated by President Lyndon B. Johnson in order to improve economic and educational

opportunities for African Americans. The federal government instituted affirmative action policies under the
landmark Civil Rights Act of 1964 and an executive order
in 1965. It consisted of policies, programs, and procedures
that gave preferences in job hiring, higher education, government contracts, and other social benefits. Businesses
receiving federal funds were prohibited from using apti-
tude tests and other criteria that tended to discriminate
against African Americans. Affirmative action programs
were monitored by the Office of Federal Contract Compliance and the EEOC. Subsequently, affirmative action
was broadened to cover women and Native Americans,
Hispanics, and other minorities and was extended to colleges and universities and state and federal agencies. The
typical criteria for affirmative action are race, disability,
gender, ethnic origin, and age.

By the late 1970s the use of racial quotas led to court
challenges of affirmative action as a form of reverse discrimination. The first major challenge was *Regents of the
University of California* v. *Bakke* (1978), in which the U.S.
Supreme Court ruled (5–4) affirmative action constitutional but invalidated the use of quotas to reserve places
for minority applicants if white applicants are denied a
chance to compete for those places; colleges could still use
race as a factor in making admissions decisions.

The Supreme Court began to impose significant
restrictions on race-based affirmative action in 1989. In a
pair of legal cases called the *Bollinger* decisions addressing

the issue of affirmative action, the U.S. Supreme Court ruled on June 23, 2003 that the undergraduate admissions policy of the University of Michigan, with its use of an automatic race-based point system used to accept new students, violated the equal-protection clause of the Fourteenth Amendment to the U.S. Constitution (*Gratz* v. *Bollinger*), while the admissions policy of the University of Michigan Law School did not (*Grutter* v. *Bollinger*). Ten years later, in *Fisher* v. *University of Texas at Austin*, the Supreme Court vacated and remanded an appeals court decision that had rejected a challenge to an affirmative action program modeled on the one approved in *Gratz*, finding that the lower court had not subjected the program to strict scrutiny, the most-demanding form of judicial review. After the appeals court upheld the program a second time, the Supreme Court affirmed that decision (2016), determining that strict scrutiny had been satisfied.

CHAPTER SEVEN

HABEAS CORPUS

Habeas corpus is an ancient common-law written order issued by a court or judge that directs someone who holds another person in his custody to produce him or her before the court. The most important way the order is used is to correct violations of personal liberty by directing judicial inquiry into the legality of a detention. The right of habeas corpus is recognized in common-law systems but generally not under civil law, although some have adopted comparable procedures.

A HISTORY OF HABEAS CORPUS

Before the Magna Carta (1215), the charter of liberties granted by King John of England, a variety of writs (written orders) performed some of the functions of habeas corpus. Habeas corpus was used during the Middle Ages to bring cases from inferior tribunals into the king's courts. The modern history of the writ as a device for the protection of personal liberty against official authority may date from the reign of Henry VII (1485–1509) of England, when efforts were made to use it on behalf of persons imprisoned by the Privy Council. By the reign of Charles I, in the 17th century, the writ was fully established as the appropriate process for checking the illegal imprisonment of people by inferior courts or public officials. Many of these rights were provided by the Habeas Corpus Act of 1679, which authorized judges to issue the writ when courts were on vacation and provided severe penalties for any judge who refused to comply with it. Its use was expanded during the 19th century to cover those held under private authority. In 1960, legislation was enacted limiting when habeas corpus could be denied and establishing new lines of appeal.

In the British colonies in North America at the time of the American Revolution, the rights to habeas corpus were regarded as basic protections of individual liberty. The U.S. Constitution guaranteed that the privilege "shall not be suspended, unless when in cases of rebellion or invasion the public safety may require it." President Abraham Lincoln suspended the writ by executive proclamation at the outbreak of the Civil War. On May 25, 1861, John Merryman was imprisoned by military order at Fort McHenry, Baltimore, Maryland, for alleged pro-Confederate activities. Supreme Court Chief Justice Roger B. Taney, sitting as a federal circuit court judge, issued a writ of habeas corpus on the grounds that Merryman was illegally detained. General George Cadwalader, commander of Fort McHenry, refused to obey the writ on the ground that President Abraham Lincoln had suspended habeas corpus. Taney, however, contended that the power of suspension resided only in Congress, citing Cadwalader for contempt of court and writing an opinion about Article I, Section 9, of the Constitution, which allows suspension of habeas corpus "when in cases of rebellion or invasion the public safety may require it." Taney argued that only Congress—not the president—had the power of suspension. Lincoln ignored the order of the court, justifying his action in a message to Congress in July 1861 and adhering to the suspension throughout the war. While Merryman was later released, the constitutional question of who has the right to suspend habeas corpus was never officially resolved, although modern opinion supports the view that suspension of the writ requires the consent of Congress.

The Supreme Court's liberal interpretation of the constitutional rights of defendants led many prisoners in the mid-20th century to file habeas corpus petitions, challenging their convictions. A writ is frequently

Abraham Lincoln was sworn in as the 16th president of the United States on March 4, 1861. Chief Justice Roger B. Taney administers the oath of office while the preceding president, James Buchanan (*far left*), looks on.

requested on behalf of one in police custody, requiring the police to either charge or release the arrested person. Habeas corpus proceedings may be employed to obtain release of the accused prior to trial on the ground that the bail set is excessive. On occasion, habeas corpus relief has been granted a prisoner who is unlawfully detained after expiration of his sentence. In cases of one arrested on a warrant of extradition, a proceeding in habeas corpus may be instituted to challenge the validity of the warrant. The writ may also be employed in a wide variety of situations not involving criminal proceedings. Competing claims to the custody of a minor may be adjudicated in habeas corpus. Persons confined to a mental hospital may in some jurisdictions bring about their release by showing at a habeas corpus hearing that they have recovered their sanity.

KOREMATSU V. *UNITED STATES*

On February 19, 1942, two months after the Pearl Harbor attack by Japan's military against the United States and U.S. entry into World War II, President Franklin D. Roosevelt issued Executive Order 9066, which enabled his secretary of war and military commanders "to prescribe military areas in such places and of such extent as he or the appropriate Military Commander may determine, from which any or all persons may be excluded." Although the order mentioned no group in particular, it subsequently was applied to most of the Japanese American population on the West Coast. Soon thereafter, the Nisei of southern California's Terminal Island were ordered to vacate their homes, leaving behind all but what they could carry. On March 18, Roosevelt signed another executive order, creating the War Relocation Authority, a civilian agency charged with speeding the process of relocating Japanese Americans. A few days later, the first wave of "evacuees" arrived at Manzanar War Relocation Center. Most spent the next three years there.

On May 3, Exclusion Order Number 34 was issued, under which 23-year-old Fred Korematsu—a son of Japanese immigrants born in Oakland, California—and his

Manzanar Relocation Center, a collection of tar-paper barracks in the desert, near Lone Pine, California, was an internment camp for Japanese Americans during World War II.

family were to be relocated. Although his family followed the order, Fred failed to submit to relocation. He was arrested on May 30 and taken to Tanforan Relocation Center, south of San Francisco. Korematsu argued that Executive Order 9066 violated his Fifth-Amendment right against deprivation of liberty without due process because the government had not suspended the right of habeas corpus. He was convicted of having violated a military order and received a sentence of five years' probation. He and his family were relocated to Topaz Internment Camp in Utah. Korematsu appealed his conviction to the U.S. Court of Appeals, which upheld the conviction and the exclusion order. The Supreme Court agreed to hear his appeal, and oral arguments were held on October 11, 1944. In a 6–3 ruling issued on December 18, the court upheld Korematsu's conviction for having violated an exclusion order requiring him to submit to forced relocation. Writing for the majority, Justice Hugo L. Black argued that while forcing citizens from their homes was normally inconsistent with U.S. constitutional principles, in situations dealing with modern warfare "the power to protect must be commensurate with the threatened danger." In 2011 it was revealed that the government had deceived the Supreme Court in the Korematsu case by suppressing a report by the Office of Naval Intelligence that concluded that Japanese Americans did not pose a threat to U.S. national security.

NISEI IN NORTH AMERICA

"Nisei," a Japanese term meaning "second-born," refers to second-generation Japanese people born in the United States. During World War II, all persons of Japanese ancestry living on the West Coast were forcibly relocated to inland detention centres as a result of hysteria following the Japanese attack on Pearl Harbor. The U.S. government claimed that it was forced by public outcry, agitation from press and radio, and military necessity to establish the War Relocation Authority and the subsequent evacuation.

Members of a Nisei unit attached to the U.S. Fifth Army can be seen passing through liberated Livorno in Italy, July 1944.

Under the jurisdiction of the Western Defense Command, during the spring and summer of 1942, 110,000 Japanese Americans (including a number who were still aliens) were placed in ten war relocation centres located in isolated areas from the Sierra Nevada to the Mississippi River. The sparsely furnished military barracks in these camps afforded meagre "work opportunities" for adults and a minimal education for children. By the time the evacuation was complete, U.S. forces were largely in command of the Pacific and all danger of a possible Japanese invasion had passed. After individual screening at the centres to prove their loyalty, 17,600 Nisei were accepted for service in the U.S. armed forces; many of their units were later cited for bravery.

Demands for redress for the losses and injury suffered by the evacuees during the war were not addressed until 1988, when the U.S. government apologized, providing partial monetary payments to the 60,000 surviving Japanese Americans who had been interned.

RASUL V. *BUSH*

The habeas corpus rights of foreign nationals have been debated in relation to prisoners of the United States held at the Guantánamo Bay detention camp on the U.S. naval base in Cuba. On June 28, 2004, in *Rasul* v. *Bush*, the U.S. Supreme Court ruled that U.S. courts have jurisdiction to hear habeas corpus petitions filed on behalf of foreign nationals imprisoned at Guantánamo because the base, which the United States has held under lease from Cuba since 1899, is effectively within U.S. territory. The decision meant that hundreds of foreign nationals held at the camp had a legal right to challenge their imprisonment.

The case originally concerned four British and Australian citizens, Shafiq Rasul, Asif Iqbal, Mamdouh Habib, and David Hicks, who had been seized in Pakistan and Afghanistan in 2001–02 and eventually turned over to U.S. authorities. The four men were transferred to the Guantánamo Bay detention camp, where they were held without charge, trial, or access to counsel. Rasul, Iqbal, and Hicks challenged their detentions in U.S. district court, arguing that they had not engaged in combat against the United States or in any terrorist acts and that their detention amounted to a violation of the due-process clause of the Fifth Amendment. Habib filed a similar suit three months later. Hearing the first case, *Rasul* v. *Bush*, together with a similar case involving twelve Kuwaiti citizens, *al Odah* v. *Bush*, the district court dismissed the challenges, holding on the basis of *Johnson* v. *Eisentrager* (1950) that foreign nationals imprisoned abroad may not file habeas corpus petitions in U.S. courts because the jurisdictions of such courts are limited to territory within the United States. The court later dismissed *Habib* v. *Bush* on the same grounds.

After these decisions were affirmed by a court of appeals, the Supreme Court granted a writ of certiorari to hear the consolidated cases as *Rasul* v. *Bush*; oral arguments were heard on April 20, 2004. While the case was pending, the petitioners Shafiq Rasul and Asif Iqbal were released from detention at Guantánamo and set free in the United Kingdom upon arrival. In a 6–3 ruling, issued on June 28, the court overturned the lower courts' decisions. Justice John Paul Stevens held that, although Cuba retains "ultimate sovereignty," the complete jurisdiction exercised by the United States over the Guantánamo Bay naval base was sufficient to guarantee habeas corpus rights to foreign nationals held there.

BOUMEDIENE V. *BUSH*

In *Boumediene* v. *Bush*, issued on June 12, 2008, the U.S. Supreme Court held that the Military Commissions Act (MCA) of 2006, which barred foreign nationals held by the United States as "enemy combatants" from challenging their detentions in U.S. federal courts, was an unconstitutional suspension of the writ of habeas corpus guaranteed in the U.S. Constitution.

In 2002 six Algerians were arrested in Bosnia and Herzegovina on suspicion of plotting to attack the U.S. embassy in Sarajevo; designated enemy combatants, they were imprisoned at the Guantánamo Bay detention camp. One of the detainees, Lakhdar Boumediene, petitioned in federal district court for a writ of habeas corpus, which was denied on the grounds that the camp was outside U.S.

territory and therefore not within the court's jurisdiction. In 2004, however, the Supreme Court had deemed in *Rasul* v. *Bush* that foreign nationals detained there were entitled to habeas corpus privileges. Foreseeing habeas corpus petitions from hundreds of foreign detainees in the camp, Congress passed the MCA, stripping the federal courts of jurisdiction to hear habeas corpus petitions on behalf of foreign detainees designated enemy combatants according to procedures established in the Detainee Treatment Act (DTA) of 2005. On the basis of the MCA, the United States Court of Appeals for the District of Columbia Circuit denied Boumediene's second appeal. The Supreme Court granted a writ of certiorari, and oral arguments were heard on December 5, 2007.

The main issue to be decided was whether the MCA violated the Suspension Clause of Article I of the Constitution, which states: "The Privilege of the Writ of Habeas Corpus shall not be suspended, unless when in Cases of Rebellion or Invasion the public Safety may require it." In a 5–4 ruling issued on June 12, 2008, the court held that the MCA did violate the Suspension Clause. In his dissenting opinion, Justice Antonin Scalia warned that the court's decision "will almost certainly cause more Americans to be killed."

CHAPTER EIGHT

THE LEGAL CONCEPT OF OBSCENITY

Obscenity is a legal concept used to characterize material as offensive to the public. Legal restrictions on the content of literature and works of visual art have existed since ancient times. While traditionally governments were concerned with seditious and heretical material, sexuality has become a major preoccupation of political and religious authorities. One of the first systematic efforts to regulate literature was undertaken by the Roman Catholic Church, which banned heretical works as early as the 4th century. Immoral works were also suppressed in Protestant countries such as England, where, prior to the 18th century, restrictions were applied almost exclusively to antireligious publications, rather than obscene material in the modern sense.

THE EMERGENCE OF OBSCENITY LAW

Modern obscenity law emerged as a direct response to social and technological changes—particularly the development of the printing press in the 15th century—that permitted the wide and easy distribution of sexually explicit material. By the 17th century, such books and prints had become widely available throughout Europe; governments and church authorities responded by arresting and prosecuting publishers and distributors. A similar sequence of events occurred in Japan, where the development of color woodblock printing created a sizable industry in erotic pictures. In 1722, the Japanese government introduced the first of several edicts against unlicensed materials, erotic and political.

In the 1720s, Edmund Curll became the first person to be convicted on a charge of obscenity in the English common-law courts for his publication of a mildly pornographic work written several decades earlier; his sentence, a fine and one hour in the pillory, was delayed because no punishment was specified in the law. Thereafter, obscenity was recognized as an indictable misdemeanor under common law. It was difficult to differentiate between the suppression of published materials for moral reasons or political repression. Thus, the 18th-century English laws that regulated indecent materials were also used to suppress criticism of government ministers and other favoured political figures. In the 1760s the journalist and politician John Wilkes, a leading government critic, was charged with seditious libel for his periodical *North Briton* and with obscene libel for his poem "An Essay on Woman," a parody of Alexander Pope's "An Essay on Man." Prosecutions for obscenity in other European countries also merged moral and political concerns. Perhaps the most celebrated obscenity trial in 19th-century France was that of Gustave Flaubert, who was charged with "outrage to public morals and religion" for his novel *Madame Bovary* (1857). The prosecution, which was unsuccessful, was motivated primarily by the government's desire to close down *Revue de Paris*, the magazine in which the work first appeared.

By the mid-19th century the spread of Victorian notions of morality resulted in harsher legislation against publication of sexually explicit material. In Great Britain, such material was prohibited on purely sexual grounds by the Obscene Publications Act of 1857. The legislation, which failed to define obscenity, was passed after the lord chief justice guaranteed it would be used to prosecute individuals for works "written for the single purpose of corrupting the morals of youth" and "to shock the common feelings of decency." A legal definition of obscenity was established by *Regina* v. *Hicklin* (1868), in which the Court of Queen's Bench held that obscene material is marked by a tendency "to deprave and corrupt those whose minds are open to such immoral influences." It was understood that this test could be applied to isolated passages of a work, and the ruling made it possible to label a work obscene not on the basis of the intended readership but on how it might influence anyone in society (e.g., women and children). This perspective formed the basis of anti-obscenity laws in legal systems influenced by British law.

OBSCENITY IN AMERICA

In the 1820s, state governments in the United States began passing obscenity laws; in 1842, the federal government enacted legislation allowing the seizure of obscene pictures. The most comprehensive federal legislation of the era was the Comstock Act (1873), which provided for the fine and imprisonment of any person mailing or receiving obscene publications. The act became the basis for widespread suppression not merely of pornographic books and pictures but also publications containing medical information about contraception and abortion.

The variability of legal definitions of obscenity is well-illustrated by court cases in the United States. Until the middle of the 20th century, the standard definition used by U.S. courts was the one articulated in the British *Hicklin* case. On this basis, several novels, including Theodore Dreiser's *An American Tragedy* (1925) and D.H. Lawrence's *Lady Chatterley's Lover* (1928), were banned. In 1934 a New York circuit court of appeals abandoned the *Hicklin* standard, legalizing the publication of James Joyce's novel *Ulysses* and holding that the proper standard for judging obscenity was not the content of isolated passages but rather "whether a publication taken as a whole has a libidinous effect." Two decades later, in *Roth* v. *United States* (1957), the U.S. Supreme Court held that the standard of obscenity should be "whether... the dominant theme of the material taken as a whole appeals to prurient interest." The court struggled to develop a more adequate definition, which is reflected in Associate Supreme Court Justice Potter Stewart's opinion in *Jacobellis* v. *Ohio* (1964). Of obscenity in a motion picture, he wrote: "I know it when I see it." In a 1966 ruling on John Cleland's novel *Fanny Hill* (1748–49), the court declared that, in order to be pornographic, a work must be "utterly without redeeming social value."

In *Miller* v. *California* (1973), the Supreme Court devised a three-part test to determine whether a work was obscene: (1) "the average person, applying contemporary community standards," would judge that the work appeals primarily to prurient interests; (2) "the work depicts or describes, in a patently offensive way, sexual conduct specifically defined by the applicable state law"; and (3) the work "lacks serious literary, artistic, political, or scientific value." Although the *Miller* decision expanded the legal basis for suppressing sexually explicit books and motion pictures, the public's increasingly permissive attitude toward issues related to sex and marriage made such prosecutions difficult to pursue in the late 20th and early 21st century.

LATER DEVELOPMENTS

Beginning in the late 1970s, a series of increasingly strict laws in the United States criminalized the possession of photographs of nude children or of children in sexually suggestive poses, though similar pictures of adults would have been deemed merely indecent. In *New York* v. *Ferber* (1982), the Supreme Court upheld the use of strict standards of obscenity in cases involving children, maintaining the government's interest in protecting children. In *Osborne* v. *Ohio* (1990), the court upheld a law that criminalized the private possession of a photograph of a nude adolescent.

Throughout the 1980s, feminist groups campaigned against pornography not because it offended traditional sexual morality but because it degraded women, violated their human rights, and encouraged sex crimes. Feminist arguments had some influence on obscenity laws in certain countries, notably Canada, which in the 1980s clamped down on pornography. The implementation of such laws pitted feminist reformers against those supporting a more libertarian approach. The feminist approach prompted some U.S. cities to pass local ordinances against pornography. However, many of these regulations were struck down by U.S. federal courts in the 1990s.

In the late 20th and early 21st century, differences between countries regarding legal definitions and cultural conceptions of obscenity became increasingly important with the development of the Internet, which enabled anyone with a computer to view materials originating from anywhere in the world. This complicated the regulation of child pornography in many jurisdictions because of differences regarding the legal definition of childhood, the legal age of sexual consent, and tolerance of suggestive or indecent images of children. Various solutions were attempted to limit access to what were considered obscene Internet sites (e.g., by requiring that libraries deny access to Web sites of a sexual nature). However, the courts in the United States showed little sympathy toward such efforts. Particularly problematic was that material considered obscene by some may be considered to have social merit by others (e.g., information about breast-cancer prevention or sex education). Countries with success in reducing access to Internet pornography (e.g., China and Saudi Arabia) adopted stringent restrictions on most Internet access. Despite these problems, there were moves in Western countries to adopt consistent policies toward child pornography, often in imitation of the United States.

ASHCROFT V. FREE SPEECH COALITION

On April 16, 2002, in *Ashcroft* v. *Free Speech Coalition*, the U.S. Supreme Court upheld a lower court's decision that provisions of the Child Pornography Prevention Act (CPPA) of 1996 were vague, overly broad, and in violation of the free-speech protection contained in the First Amendment. The act specifically prohibited computer-generated or altered depictions of minors engaging in explicit sexual conduct and images of explicit sexual conduct by adults who resemble minors. The court ruled that an expanded definition of child pornography including any image that "appears to be" of a minor engaging in sexually explicit conduct would criminalize images that are not obscene nor produced with children.

The CPPA was introduced in the U.S. Congress in response to the development of computer technology that allowed the creation of images that appeared to be photographs of real subjects but were entirely artificial. Other technology enabled genuine photographs to be digitally altered, introducing virtually undetectable fictional elements. The sponsors of the legislation argued that the existing legal definition of child pornography as images of minors engaged in explicit sexual conduct needed to be broadened to include computer-generated or altered images. They reasoned that such images could be used as easily by pedophiles to seduce children into sexual conduct, that they were just as effective in whetting the pedophile's desire to exploit children sexually, and that their similarity to real images would make it difficult to identify and prosecute those who possessed or distributed child pornography. The Free

A young protester stands outside the U.S. Supreme Court building in Washington, D.C., in a demonstration against child pornography on the Internet, March 19, 1997.

Speech Coalition, a trade association of the adult entertainment industry, filed suit in federal district court, which found in favour of the government.

The decision was later reversed by the Ninth Circuit

CHILD PORNOGRAPHY AS DEFINED IN THE CCPA

The CCPA defined child pornography as "any visual depiction, including any photograph, film, video, picture, or computer or computer-generated image or picture...of sexually explicit conduct," in which:

(A) the production of such visual depiction involves the use of a minor engaging in sexually explicit conduct;

(B) such visual depiction is, or appears to be, of a minor engaging in sexually explicit conduct;

(C) such visual depiction has been created, adapted, or modified to appear that an identifiable minor is engaging in sexually explicit conduct; or

(D) such visual depiction is advertised, promoted, presented, described, or distributed in such a manner that conveys the impression that the material is or contains a visual depiction of a minor engaging in sexually explicit conduct.

Court of Appeals. The Supreme Court granted a writ of certiorari, and oral arguments were heard on October 30, 2001. In a 6–3 ruling issued on April 16, 2002, the court upheld the Ninth Circuit's decision. Writing for the majority, Justice Anthony M. Kennedy argued that the CPPA would prohibit speech that is clearly not obscene by the definition established in *Miller* v. *California* (1973)— that a work is obscene if, taken as a whole, it appeals to prurient sexual interests, is patently offensive by community standards, and is devoid of literary, artistic, political, or scientific value. He also rejected the government's analogy with *New York* v. *Ferber*, in which the court found that even speech that was not obscene could be banned in order to protect children from being sexually exploited in its production. Unlike the child pornography prohibited in *Ferber*, the virtual child pornography banned by the CPPA "records no crime and

William Rehnquist, 1976.

creates no victims by its production. . . . While the Government asserts that the images can lead to actual instances of child abuse, the causal link is contingent and indirect." Chief Justice William Rehnquist dissented from the majority, arguing that the majority had construed the CCPA too broadly and that it was never the intention of Congress to prohibit speech of genuine merit, such as that of a modern film portraying the teenage lovers in Shakespeare's Romeo and Juliet.

CHAPTER NINE

PRIVACY AND REPRODUCTIVE RIGHTS

Although the U.S. Constitution does not explicitly protect privacy, the right is commonly regarded as created by certain provisions, particularly the First, Fourth, and Fifth amendments. The Fourth Amendment prohibits unreasonable searches and seizures; the First and Fifth include privacy protections, in that they focus not on what the government may do but rather on the individual's freedom to be autonomous.

RIGHTS OF PRIVACY

Rights of privacy are an amalgam of principles in U.S. law, embodied in the federal Constitution or recognized by courts or lawmaking bodies, concerning what Supreme Court Justice Louis Brandeis described in 1890 as "the right to be left alone." The right of privacy is a legal concept in both the law of torts (the branch of civil law generally concerned with harmful or injurious behaviour) and U.S. constitutional law. The tort concept is of 19th-century origin.

Subject to limitations of public policy, it asserts a right of persons to recover damages or obtain injunctive relief for unjustifiable invasions of privacy prompted by motives of gain, curiosity, or malice. In torts law, privacy is a right not to be disturbed emotionally by conduct designed to subject the victim to great tensions by baring his intimate life and affairs to public view or by humiliating and annoying invasions of his solitude. Less broad protections of privacy are afforded public officials and other prominent persons considered to be "public figures," as defined by law.

The rights of privacy were initially interpreted to include only protection against tangible intrusions resulting in measurable injury. After publication of an influential article by Justice Brandeis and Samuel Warren, "The Right to Privacy," in the *Harvard Law Review* in 1890, the federal courts began to explore various constitutional principles that today are regarded as constituent elements of a constitutional right to privacy. For example, in 1923 the Supreme Court struck down a Nebraska law prohibiting schools from teaching any language other than English, saying the law interfered with the rights of personal autonomy. In 1965 the Supreme Court held that the federal Constitution included an implied right of privacy. In that case, *Griswold* v. *Connecticut*, the court invalidated a law prohibiting the use of contraceptives, even by married persons. Justice William O. Douglas, writing for the court, stated that there is a "zone of privacy" within a "penumbra" created by fundamental constitutional guarantees, including the First, Fourth, and Fifth amendments. The Supreme Court extended this right to privacy to sexual relationships in 2003, striking down a Texas law criminalizing sodomy.

The "right to be left alone" also has been extended to provide the individual with at least some control over information about himself, including files kept by schools, employers, credit bureaus, and government agencies. Under the U.S. Privacy Act of 1974, individuals are guaranteed access to many government files pertaining to themselves, and the agencies of government that maintain such files are prohibited from disclosing personal information except under court order and certain other limited circumstances. In 2001 the USA PATRIOT Act (formally, the Uniting and Strengthening America by Providing Appropriate Tools Required to Intercept and Obstruct Terrorism Act of 2001) granted federal police agencies the authority to search the business records of individuals it suspected of involvement in terrorism, including their library records. Modern technology, giving rise to electronic eavesdropping, and the practices of industrial espionage have complicated the problem of maintaining a right of privacy in both tort and constitutional law. On June 2, 2015, President Barack Obama signed the Senate-approved USA Freedom Act into law, which replaced the USA PATRIOT Act and curtailed the government's authority to collect data. This revision was largely in response to Edward Snowden's exposure in 2013

President George W. Bush signing the USA PATRIOT Act in the East Room of the White House, Washington, D.C., October 26, 2001.

of the government's bulk collection of phone and Internet records. The USA Freedom Act stipulated that the government can access such data only after submitting public requests to the FISA Court.

GRISWOLD V. STATE OF CONNECTICUT

On June 7, 1965, in *Griswold* v. *State of Connecticut*, the U.S. Supreme Court found in favour of the constitutional right of married persons to use birth control. The state case was originally ruled in favour of the plaintiff, the state of

Connecticut. Estelle Griswold, the executive director of the Planned Parenthood League of Connecticut, and Lee Buxton, a physician and professor at Yale Medical School who served as Medical Director for the League, were convicted as accessories to the crime of providing married couples information about contraception and in some cases writing prescriptions for contraceptive devices for the woman. At the time of their arrests (1961), Connecticut law made it a crime for any person to use a device or drug to prevent conception, and it was also a crime for any person to assist, abet, counsel, cause, or command another to do the same. The defendants were found guilty of such assistance and fined $100 each.

In its judgment, the Supreme Court ruled that Connecticut's birth control law was unconstitutional based on rights set down in the Fourth and Fifth amendments that protect an individual's home and private life from interference by the government. Judging marriage to be a sacred and private bond that lies within a zone of privacy guaranteed by several provisions within the constitution, namely the concept of liberty implied in the Bill of Rights, the Court found that the original decision against Griswold and Buxton should be overturned, and that citizens in the state of Connecticut (and, effectively, throughout the country) should enjoy the freedom to use birth control within the bounds of marriage. This particular privacy case has been cited in other important Supreme Court judgments, including *Roe* v. *Wade* (1973) and *Planned Parenthood of Southeastern Pennsylvania* v. *Casey* (1992).

ABORTION

Abortion is the expulsion of a fetus from the uterus before it has reached the stage of viability (in human beings, usually about the 20th week of gestation). An abortion may occur spontaneously, in which case it is also called a miscarriage, or it may be brought on purposefully, in which case it is often called an induced abortion. Abortion was a common and socially accepted method of family limitation in the Greco-Roman world. Although Christian theologians early and vehemently condemned abortion, the application of severe criminal sanctions to deter its practice became common only in the 19th century. In the late 20th century China used abortion on a large scale as part of its population-control policy. In the early 21st century, some jurisdictions with large Roman Catholic populations decriminalized abortion despite strong opposition from the church. Public debate surrounding the topic of abortion has demonstrated the enormous difficulties experienced by political institutions in grappling with the complex and ambiguous ethical problems raised by the issue. Opponents of abortion, or of abortion for any reason other than to save the life of the mother, argue that there is no rational basis for distinguishing the fetus from a newborn infant; each is totally dependent and potentially a member of society, and each possesses a degree of humanity. Proponents of liberalized regulation of abortion hold that only a woman herself, rather than the state, has the right to manage her pregnancy and that the alternative to legal, medically supervised abortion is illegal and demonstrably dangerous, if not deadly, abortion.

A broad social movement for the relaxation or elimination of restrictions on the performance of abortions resulted in the passing of liberalized legislation in several states in the United States during the 1960s. The U.S. Supreme Court ruled in *Roe* v. *Wade* (1973) that unduly restrictive state regulation of abortion was unconstitutional, in effect legalizing abortion for any reason for women in the first three months of pregnancy. In a 7–2 vote on January 22, the Supreme Court upheld the lower court's decision that a Texas statute criminalizing abortion in most instances violated a woman's constitutional right of privacy, which the court found implicit in the liberty guarantee of the due-process clause of the Fourteenth Amendment. The case began in 1970 when Jane Roe (an alias of Norma McCorvey) instituted federal action against Henry Wade, the district attorney of Dallas county, Texas, where Roe resided. The court disagreed with Roe's assertion of an absolute right to terminate her pregnancy in any way and at any time and attempted to balance a woman's right of privacy with a state's interest in regulating abortion. The court stated that only a "compelling state interest" justifies regulations limiting "fundamental rights," such as privacy, and that legislators must therefore draw statutes narrowly "to express the legitimate state interests at stake." The court attempted to balance the state's distinct interests in the health of pregnant women and in the potential life of fetuses. It placed the point after which a state's compelling interest in the pregnant woman's health would allow it to regulate abortion "at approximately the end of the first trimester" of pregnancy. With regard to fetuses, the court located that point at "capability for meaningful life outside the mother's womb," or viability. The court held that the Texas statute was unconstitutional because of its breadth.

PLANNED PARENTHOOD OF SOUTHEASTERN PENNSYLVANIA V. CASEY

In 1992, in *Planned Parenthood of Southeastern Pennsylvania v. Casey*, the U.S. Supreme Court redefined several provisions regarding abortion rights as established in *Roe* v. *Wade*.

In 1988 and 1989 the Commonwealth of Pennsylvania, led by Governor Robert Casey, enacted new abortion statutes that required that a woman seeking an abortion give her informed consent, that a minor seeking an abortion obtain parental consent (the provision included a judicial waiver option), that a married woman notify her husband of her intended abortion, and, finally, that clinics provide certain information to a woman seeking an abortion and

ABORTION AND OBAMACARE

The Patient Protection and Affordable Care Act (PPACA), also called the Affordable Care Act (ACA) or "Obamacare," was widely considered the most far-reaching health care reform act since the passage of Medicare, the U.S. government program guaranteeing health insurance for the elderly, in 1965. Signed into law by President Barack Obama in March 2010, with provisions that required most individuals to secure health insurance or pay fines, PPACA made coverage easier and less costly to obtain, cracked down on abusive insurance practices, and attempted to rein in rising costs of health care. Compromise on abortion language in the act aided passage of the House of Representatives' initial version of the bill, because some conservative pro-life Democrats, including Bart Stupak of Michigan, threatened to withhold support unless language were added restricting coverage of abortion in any health insurance plan that received federal subsidies. Abortion once again threatened to derail the legislation in the Senate, since Stupak and a group of pro-life Democrats objected to the Senate language on abortion, but Obama intervened by pledging to issue an executive order clarifying that federal money could not be used to provide abortions. By December 24, 2009, both the House of Representatives and the Senate had

The Affordable Care Act imposed limitations on the use of federal money. Under the reform law, federal funds could not be used for abortions except in cases of rape or incest or when the mother's life was endangered.

passed versions of the legislation, which would provide health care to more than 30 million uninsured Americans. In a ruling issued in June 2012, the U.S. Supreme Court held (5–4) that the individual mandate (the requirement that most Americans obtain health insurance by January 1, 2014 or pay a fine) was constitutional under Congress's taxing power and that the law's expansion of Medicaid (the national health-insurance program for the poor, jointly funded by the federal government and the states) was constitutional as long as states that refused to expand their Medicaid rolls did not lose federal Medicaid funding for existing beneficiaries.

wait twenty-four hours before performing the abortion. Before any of these laws could take effect, Planned Parenthood of Southeastern Pennsylvania brought suit against the governor, challenging the constitutionality of the statutes.

In a 1992 plurality opinion, the U.S. Supreme Court affirmed the "essential holding" (i.e., the basic principle)

Police officers look out from a Planned Parenthood clinic in downtown Washington, D.C., after an explosive device detonated nearby on January 22, 1997. Thousands of antiabortion demonstrators came together on the anniversary of the *Roe* v. *Wade* Supreme Court decision, which legalized abortion.

of *Roe* v. *Wade*, that women have a right to choose abortion prior to fetal viability, but rejected Roe's trimester-based framework for allowing states to curb the availability of abortion in favour of a more flexible medical definition of viability. The decision restated that the source of the privacy right that undergirds women's right to choose abortion derives from the due-process clause of the Fourteenth Amendment, placing individual decisions about abortion, family planning, marriage, and education within "a realm of personal liberty which the government may not enter." The judgment also revised the test that courts use to scrutinize laws relating to abortion, moving to an "undue burden" standard: a law is invalid if its "purpose or effect is to place substantial obstacles in the path of a woman seeking an abortion before the fetus attains viability." Ultimately, the court upheld all the provisions of the Pennsylvania statute under attack except for the requirement of spousal notification. Many suits brought since have centred on the meaning of "undue burden." In *Whole Woman's Health* v. *Hellerstedt* (2016), the court invalidated two provisions of a 2013 Texas law that had imposed strict requirements on abortion clinics in the state, purportedly in the interest of protecting women's health. The court ruled that the two provisions placed an "impermissible obstacle" to women seeking an abortion in Texas, in violation of the court's decision in *Planned Parenthood* v. *Casey*.

CHAPTER TEN

SAME-SEX MARRIAGE AND THE LAW

Societies have resolved the intertwined issues of sexuality, reproduction, and marriage in many ways. Their responses regarding the morality, desirability, and administrative benefits of same-sex partnerships have been equally diverse. By the beginning of the 21st century, most countries opted for one of only three legal resolutions: to ignore same-sex partnerships, to criminalize them, or to grant them a status similar or equal to that of heterosexual marriage.

LEGAL RESOLUTIONS

Many societies and jurisdictions have chosen to ignore or actively criminalize the issue of same-sex marriage, contending that homosexuality and lesbianism are mental disorders. These cultures moved same-sex intimacy and marriage from the realm of civil regulations (the domain of contract law) to that of public safety (the domain of criminal law). In such societies, the possibility of arrest or institutionalization further reinforced taboos on same-sex intimacy and discussions thereof, typically driving such activities underground. In the early 21st century, the countries that most seriously penalized same-sex relations tended to be in deeply conservative regions of the world, particularly Islamic theocracies and some parts of Asia and Africa. They often proscribed behaviours that other countries viewed as subject to moral, rather than legal, regulation. The judicial systems of many predominantly Muslim countries, for instance, invoke Islamic law (Sharīʿah) in a wide range of contexts. A variety of sexual or quasi-sexual acts, usually including same-sex intimacy, were criminalized in these countries, and the penalties for these acts could be as severe as execution. However, Iranian Ayatollah Ruhollah Khomeini issued a legal decree, or fatwa, supporting gender reassignment surgery when undertaken by individuals who wished to "fix" their physiology and thus become heterosexual in the eyes of the law.

In contrast, the acceptance of same-sex partnerships was particularly apparent in northern Europe and in countries with cultural ties to that region. In 1989 Denmark became the first country to establish registered partnerships—an attenuated version of marriage—for same-sex couples. Many nearby countries followed suit, using specific vocabulary (e.g., civil union, civil partnership, domestic partnership, registered partnership) to differentiate same-sex unions from heterosexual marriages. By the early 21st century, this trend had spread to other European countries. Outside Europe, some jurisdictions also adopted some form of same-sex partnership rights; Israel recognized common-law same-sex marriage in the mid-1990s (the Israeli Supreme Court further ruled in 2006 that same-sex marriages performed abroad should be recognized). In 2007, Uruguay became the first Latin American country to legalize same-sex civil unions; the legislation became effective in 2008.

Some jurisdictions opted to specifically apply the honorific of "marriage" to same-sex as well as heterosexual unions. In 2001 The Netherlands revised its same-sex partnership law and became the first country to replace civil unions with marriages. In 2003, the European Union mandated that all of its members pass laws recognizing the same-sex marriages of fellow EU countries. As countries began to legalize same-sex partnerships, public opinion, particularly in Europe, began to shift in favour of full marriage rights for same-sex unions. By the mid-2000s a Eurobarometer poll (carried out by the European Commission) found that four-fifths of the citizens of The Netherlands felt that same-sex marriage should be legal throughout Europe; in a further seven countries, a majority held a similar view. However, in central and southern Europe, support for same-sex marriage remained quite low, often with less than one-fifth of those polled favouring legalization. In the United States, a majority opposed same-sex marriage rights, with only two-fifths of the population supporting legalization by the mid-2000s.

STEPS TOWARD MARRIAGE EQUALITY IN THE UNITED STATES

The question of whether couples of the same sex should be allowed to marry has roiled U.S. politics since at least 1993. In that year, the Supreme Court of Hawaii heard a case in which the plaintiffs claimed that the state's refusal to issue marriage licenses to same-sex couples abrogated those individuals' rights to equal treatment under the law; the state, in turn, argued that practice would inherently damage the public good. The court found for the plaintiffs, basing its argument on the law's absence of a clear definition of who might participate in such a partnership. In response, Hawaiian legislators added such a definition to the state constitution, nullifying the issuing of marriage licenses to same-sex partners. Many Americans felt that the Hawaii court decision represented a serious threat to social stability, and in 1996 the U.S. Congress enacted the Defense of Marriage Act. This legislation declared that same-sex marriages would not be recognized for federal purposes, such as the award of Social Security benefits normally afforded to a surviving spouse, or employment-based benefits for the partners of federal employees. The act also restated existing law by providing that no U.S. state or territory was required to recognize marriages from elsewhere. Within a decade of the federal act's passage, almost all states had enacted laws or constitutional amendments declaring that marriage was legally defined as a heterosexual institution, that same-sex marriages from other states would not be recognized, or that same-sex marriage was contrary to the public policies of the state.

Against the tide, some states moved toward the legal recognition of same-sex partnerships. In 1999 the Vermont Supreme Court declared that same-sex couples were entitled under the state constitution the same legal rights as married heterosexual couples; shortly thereafter, the state legislature enacted the Vermont Civil Union Act, conferring all the rights and responsibilities of marriage except recognition by employers for insurance coverage, and the label. In 2003, California enacted a similar statute, calling the relationships "domestic partnerships." Also in 2003, the Massachusetts Supreme Court ruled that the denial of marriage licenses to same-sex couples violated the state constitution; the court gave the state six months to comply with its order to remedy the situation. The state soon began to issue marriage licenses for same-sex couples, but these were challenged and their legal status remained uncertain. Officials in some smaller jurisdictions, notably San Francisco, joined the controversy in early 2004 by issuing marriage licenses in defiance of local prohibitions; these licenses were later found to be invalid. In 2005–07 several other states, including Connecticut, New Jersey, and New Hampshire also established same-sex civil unions, while other states and Washington, D.C., adopted jurisdiction-wide policies that accorded some spousal rights to same-sex couples. In 2008 and 2009, the supreme courts of Connecticut and Iowa ruled that their state's ban on same-sex marriage was unconstitutional. In 2009 the Vermont legislature fully legalized same-sex marriage, bringing the total to four.

THE COMPLEXITY OF THE DEBATE

Part of the complexity of the issue of same-sex marriage is that it really involves two different debates. The administrative debate, about which relationships ought to have legal consequences, was settled in the United States in 2015, when the Supreme Court ruled that state bans on same-sex marriage were unconstitutional.

The normative debate, which contains religious dimensions for many people, concerns what relationships are intrinsically valuable. The question is one about objective moral reality: are same-sex relationships morally equal to heterosexual relationships, or do heterosexual relationships partake of a good that homosexual relationships cannot possibly share? On this issue, Americans are divided, with different groups adhering to two very different moral visions. According to the anti-same-sex-marriage vision, sex can only be morally worthy because of its place in procreation. Even the marriages of infertile heterosexual couples take their meaning from the fact that they form a union of the procreative kind. From this perspective, the

OBERGEFELL V. HODGES

On June 26, 2015, in the legal case *Obergefell* v. *Hodges*, the U.S. Supreme Court ruled 5–4 that state bans on same-sex marriage and on recognizing same-sex marriages duly performed in other jurisdictions are unconstitutional under the due process and equal protection clauses of the Fourteenth Amendment. The two questions presented by the case—the constitutionality of same-sex marriage bans (the marriage question) and the constitutionality of bans on recognizing same-sex marriages (the recognition question)—were among various issues jointly presented in several related cases heard by a three-judge panel of the United States Court of Appeals for the Sixth Circuit in August 2014. In a single opinion issued in November, the panel held that the Fourteenth Amendment as well as the Supreme Court's own precedents were consistent with state laws and constitutional amendments that defined marriage as a legal relation between one man and one woman only or that denied legal effect to same-sex marriages performed out-of-state. The plaintiffs in the cases immediately filed for certiorari with the Supreme Court, which was granted in a consolidated case in January 2015. Oral arguments were heard on April 28.

Justice Anthony Kennedy asserted that the right to marry is a fundamental right "inherent in the liberty of the person" and is therefore pro-

Rainbow-colored lights shone on the White House to celebrate the U.S. Supreme Court ruling in favour of same-sex marriage on June 26, 2015, in Washington, D.C.

tected by the due process clause, which prohibits the states from depriving any person of "life, liberty, or property without due process of law." By virtue of the close connection between liberty and equality, the marriage right is also guaranteed by the equal protection clause, which forbids the states from "deny[ing] to any person... the equal protection of the laws." Kennedy also argued that the fundamental rights to marriage "apply with equal force to same-sex couples," giving them liberty to exercise those rights.

movement for same-sex marriage is a misguided attempt to deny fundamental moral distinctions. According to the other moral vision, sex is valuable, either in itself or because it draws people toward friendship of a singular degree and kind. This bringing together of persons has intrinsic worth, whether or not it leads to childbearing or child rearing. On this account, sexuality is linked to the flourishing of the next generation only to the extent that it is one of a number of factors that can bond adults together into stable familial units in which children are likely to thrive. From this perspective, it is the devaluation of same-sex intimacy that is immoral, because it reflects arbitrary and irrational discrimination.

CONCLUSION

Every so often, there comes along a judiciary case in the United States that feels so decisive—perhaps in its scale or by its sensationalism through media attention—it can be difficult to remember that the judicial branch is just one part in a tricameral system (along with the executive branch and the legislative branch) and that after a court decision has been made, it may or may not require enforcement. In fact, the judiciary has been described as the least-dangerous branch of government because it has "neither the purse nor the sword." In many cases, the parties accept the judgment of the court and conform their behaviour to it, but in others, a court must order a party to cease a particular activity. The enforcement of such orders is carried out by the executive branch and may require funding from the legislative branch. When it comes down to it, however, enforcement of the orders of any government institution depends on the enforcing institution's acceptance of the issuing institution's right to make the ruling and to have it enforced and the public's fundamental respect for the issuing body itself.

GLOSSARY

ADJUDICATION The act of a court in making a judgment or decree.

AMALGAM A mixture or combination.

APPELLATE Possessing the authority to review appeals.

ARBITRATION The process by which a disagreement is settled by a person or persons chosen by the disputing parties.

BICAMERAL Consisting of two legislative bodies.

COERCION Intimidation or force used to gain compliance.

DE FACTO Exercising power as if legally constituted or authorized; resulting from economic or social factors rather than from laws or actions of the state.

EFFICACIOUS Effective as a means to an end; capable of having the desired result.

EXPOSITOR A person who expounds or gives a presentation or explanation of a view.

HABEAS CORPUS A protection against unjust imprisonment which requires a person to be brought before a judge or court for the purpose of being formally charged or released.

IDEOLOGUE A strong and often blindly partisan advocate of a given ideology or theory of politics or society.

INJUNCTION A judicial order to do or not do something.

JURISPRUDENCE A body or system of law; the philosophy of law.

JUSTICIABLE Something that can be appropriately settled by a court.

MAXIM A saying.

PERFUNCTORY Superficial; performed merely in a routine manner.

PLAINTIFF One who brings a legal action in a court.

SEDITIOUS Tending to incite resistance to or insurrection against lawful authority.

SOVEREIGN One who exercises supreme political authority in a given realm; sovereignty.

STARE DECISIS The doctrine that the rules or principles laid down in previous court cases should be followed in all subsequent court cases in which the basic facts are the same.

WRIT OF CERTIORARI An order issued by a superior court for the reexamination of an action of a lower court; an order issued by an appellate court to obtain information on a pending case.

WRIT OF MANDAMUS An order issued by a higher court to a lower court or government official compelling the performance of a duty.

BIBLIOGRAPHY

SUPREME COURT JUSTICES

The standard biography is Albert Bushnell Hart, *Salmon Portland Chase* (1899, reissued as *Salmon P. Chase*, 1980). Frederick J. Blue, *Salmon P. Chase* (1987), is also of interest.

The only full-scale biography is William Garrott Brown, *The Life of Oliver Ellsworth* (1905). R. Lettieri, *Connecticut's Young Man of Revolution: Oliver Ellsworth* (1978), is helpful in understanding Ellsworth's early career. Gulian Verplanck, "Biographical Sketch of Chief Justice Ellsworth," *Analectic Magazine*, 3:382–403 (1814), is a useful sketch by an acquaintance of Ellsworth's. Two good modern articles are William R. Casto, "Oliver Ellsworth's Calvinism: A Biographical Essay on Religion and Political Psychology in the Early Republic," *Journal of Church and State*, 35:507–525 (1994), and "I Have Sought the Felicity and Glory of Your Administration," *Journal of Supreme Court History*, 2:73–90 (1996). Ellsworth's service in the first federal Congress is chronicled in Charlene Bangs Bickford et al. (eds.), *Documentary History of the First Federal Congress of the United States* (1972–). Ellsworth's service on the Supreme Court is described in William R. Casto, *The Supreme Court in the Early Republic* (1995); and in Maeva Marcus et al. (eds.), *Documentary History of the Supreme Court of the United States, 1789–1800* (1985).

Frank Monaghan, *John Jay* (1935, reissued 1972), is a well-written biography. Richard B. Morris, *Witnesses at the Creation: Hamilton, Madison, Jay, and the Constitu-*

tion (1985), characterizes the three men and analyzes the events surrounding the writing of the *Federalist* papers.

Although dated, still useful biographies of Marshall include Albert J. Beveridge, *The Life of John Marshall*, 4 vol. (1916–19, reprinted 1997); and James Bradley Thayer, *John Marshall* (1901, reprinted 1974). More recent biographies include Charles Hobson, *The Great Chief Justice: John Marshall and the Rule of Law* (1996); Jean Edward Smith, *John Marshall: Definer of a Nation* (1998); and Kent E. Newmyer, *John Marshall and the Heroic Age of the Supreme Court* (2001). Gerald Gunther (ed.), *John Marshall's Defense of McCulloch v. Maryland* (1969), analyzes Marshall's decision in the famous case. Marshall's writings are collected in Charles F. Hobsonet al. (eds.), *The Papers of John Marshall* (1974–).

C.B. Swisher, *Roger B. Taney* (1935, reprinted 1961), a definitive biography; Felix Frankfurter, *The Commerce Clause Under Marshall, Taney and Waite* (1937); A.J. Schumacher, *Thunder on Capitol Hill: The Life of Chief Justice Roger B. Taney* (1964), a juvenile biography with emphasis on Taney as a political figure; Samuel Tyler, *Memoir of Roger Brooke Taney, LL.D.*, 2nd rev. ed. (1876; first ed. [1872] reprinted 1970), contains Taney's autobiography and an appendix of legal opinions, including that of the Dred Scott case; A. Dunham and P.B. Kurland (eds.), *Mr. Justice*, rev. ed. (1964), and K.B. Umbreit, *Our Eleven Chief Justices: A History of the Supreme Court in Terms of Their Personalities*, vol. 1 (1938, reprinted 1969), collections of biographical essays with analyses of the contributions of chief justices to the development of the Supreme Court.

FAMOUS CASES

Harvey Fireside, *Separate and Unequal: Homer Plessy and the Supreme Court Decision That Legalized Racism* (2004); Williamjames Hull Hoffer, *Plessy v. Ferguson: Race and Inequality in Jim Crow America* (2012); Gerald J. Postema (ed.), *Racism and the Law: The Legacy and Lessons of Plessy* (1997), a collection of essays by philosophers and legal scholars; *Plessy v. Ferguson: A Brief History with Documents* (1997), ed. and with an introduction by Brook Thomas.

Don E. Fehrenbacher, *The Dred Scott Case: Its Significance in American Law and Politics* (1978); Walter Ehrlich, *They Have No Rights: Dred Scott's Struggle for Freedom* (1979); Paul Finkelman, *Dred Scott v. Sandford: A Brief History with Documents* (1997); Austin Allen, *Origins of the Dred Scott Case: Jacksonian Jurisprudence and the Supreme Court, 1837–1857* (2006); Mark A. Graber, *Dred Scott and the Problem of Constitutional Evil* (2006); David Thomas Konig, Paul Finkelman, and Christopher Alan Bracey (eds.), *The Dred Scott Case: Historical and Contemporary Perspectives on Race and Law* (2010).

INDEX